# Praise for *The Reading Gap:*
## *Journey to Answers*

John's book brilliantly describes the all-encompassing scope of illiteracy and sub-literacy, its far reaching consequences, and its effect on our society as a whole. I felt heartache for the unnecessary troubles faced by a single boy who wasn't taught to read and a sense of shock and dismay as the book pieced together the short bridge between illiteracy and large global issues such as crime, mental health, and basic human rights.

It is clear that the lack of proper, effective reading instruction in our schools is creating an epidemic that can no longer be ignored. Luckily, John's book also brings us hope. Hope that it is never too late to learn to read and hope that there is in fact a cure to the widespread disease known as illiteracy and sub-literacy. It's time that each and every one of us finds our voice and promotes the importance of teaching the world to read!

*Molly Woodworth, Parent*

After reading his book, I would describe John as an individual who has not only found his voice, but much more importantly, found his inner peace though his journey of vulnerability giving him the freedom to step up on his bully pulpit and demonstrate the type of courage it will take to give everyone in our nation an opportunity to learn how to read.

*Mark Thomas*
*High School Principal*
*Northview High School*
*Grand Rapids, MI*

John's book brings the reading war on research, teacher training, and instruction to the forefront explaining that teachers need to be properly trained, NOT BLAMED. Literacy is a human right and it becomes a crime when it is denied. There is no more time for excuses.

*Amy Siracusano, MS Ed.*
*Literacy Integration Specialist*
*Calvert County Public Schools*
*Maryland*

*The Reading Gap: A Journey To Answers* is a must-read for parents, teachers, and anyone interested in our educational system today or solving the widespread reading problem in our country. John Corcoran, whose story I knew, moved me more than ever with his candid tale of pain and redemption. It should thrill anyone looking for answers to discover a new and effective solution to fix this long term problem in our schools.

*Marion Zola,*
*A member of The Writer's Guild of America*

John tells us how to close the gap between what we know and what we do. With so much messaging, so much hype, and so many products and causes, it takes a special person—one who has been there, stayed there, collected information along the way while being there, and processed that information and accessed every part of his being—to state the truth about the problem and share solutions and vision in a way that is inspiring and, yes, achievable.

*Jose L. Cruz, President*
*San Diego Council on Literacy*
*Board Member. ProLiteracy*

As a literacy professional with 30 years of experience working in a library-based adult and family literacy program, I have witnessed the devastating emotional, spiritual, and economic costs of low literacy on the men and women who have stepped forward to ask for help with basic reading. I found John Corcoran's new book a provocative, galvanizing must-read for anyone who cares about literacy education in America. I could not put the book down. John's manifesto is not just a call to action for educators, but a call to action for us all.

*Valerie Hardie*
*Literacy Program Administrator*
*Southern California*

I will never forget my son's first week of fourth grade. I was volunteering at his school. I sat in the back of the room sorting papers and watching. I wasn't there an hour before I realized that my son was in trouble. He could not read. How could I not have known? How could I have let this happen? I left school, tears streaming down my face. He, at nine years old, was convinced that he was "the dumbest kid in the whole school."

My heart ached for him. We found EBLI and he learned how to read. He started the ninth grade at a ninth grade reading level.

*The Reading Gap* is a brilliant book and should be read by all who want to help ensure an equal opportunity in the classroom and workplace for all.

*Kathy Kujat*
*A proud and thankful mother of the*
*"ex-dumbest kid in the whole school"*

Pope John Paul II's 1995 message, emphasizing that literacy and education are an essential duty and investment for humanity's future, sums up the value of John Corcoran's work of the last 30 years.

Corcoran's latest book settles any debate. We have the research and anecdotal proof that we are unnecessarily damaging children and adults by failing to effectively teach reading.

This is not only academic child abuse, it is criminal destruction of lives.

*Connie Messina*
*Public High School,*
*Teacher and Counselor*

I have known John Corcoran for 35 years. I have never had a conversation with him that didn't include education and literacy. Like a general trying to win a war to save the nation, the stakes are high.

The motto of one of the John Corcoran Foundation's campaigns was "leave no one behind." The foundation enlisted one of my company's trucks to deliver computers to school children. The contract required that the students complete an on-line reading course and then they would get to keep their computers. The student was given an opportunity to learn to read and the entire family got a window into the computer world.

I hope this book inspires others to take up the literacy cause.

*Mike Robinson*
*School Board Member*
*Kings County, California Board of Education*

John Corcoran systematically communicates his personal journey of transcending from sub-literacy into literacy activism. In his generous forgiveness of an educational system that let him, as well as others, down, John claims educators didn't know then what we do now. After more than 30 years as an elementary school teacher and school administrator, I can attest that educators must intentionally look beyond teacher preparation and the teaching manual and curriculum guides if there is any hope to close the literacy gap.

His book is a call to action for each and every teacher to believe in the capacity of every student to learn at high levels and to take personal responsibility in providing instruction and interventions to that end. It is not next year's teacher, the special education teacher, or interventionist's responsibility to teach Johnny to read, it is mine!

*Julie VanBergen*
*Elementary school principal and teacher*

# THE READING GAP

## JOURNEY TO ANSWERS

# THE READING GAP

JOURNEY TO ANSWERS

# JOHN CORCORAN

The author of *"the teacher who couldn't read"*

Brehon Publishing Company
Oceanside, California

The Reading Gap: Journey to Answers
Copyright © 2017 by John Corcoran. All rights reserved.

**Published by**
Brehon Publishing Company
Oceanside, California

JohnCorcoranFoundation.org

The design, content, editorial accuracy, and views expressed or implied in this work are those of the author.

**Permission** should be addressed in writing to Brehon Publishing at mertes.c@jcfprogram.com.

Library of Congress Control Number: 2017959851

ISBN: 978-1-938620-50-8

# Dedication

*Texas Western College*
*The University of Texas at El Paso*
*The Students and Alumni*
*Dr. Diana Natalicio, President*

# Contents

# Preface

*by Maria Murray, Ph.D*

For the last two decades, I have taught both young and old how to read. I have taught educators how to teach their students to read. I have taught parents how to teach their children to read. I have taught reading in classrooms, in a university research lab, in a hockey rink, and at my kitchen table. I have published articles about reading intervention and presented research at conferences. Through it all, I have witnessed a lot of crying. Tears of children who weep from frustration, silent tears of parents who cry out of heartbreak, tears of anger from adults who learn to read too late, and tears from teachers—anxious when what they try fails to work, distressed to discover there was more they could have done.

My Ph.D. in Reading Education has afforded me the perfect job at SUNY Oswego teaching literacy instruction and assessment. My passion for the prevention and remediation of reading difficulty comes from witnessing the social, emotional, psychological, and financial ramifications of not learning to read. Little prepared me for meeting John Corcoran, whose unique and powerful story exemplifies the failures and successes that exist in literacy instruction. He visited our campus in upstate New York years ago, and has since Skyped with my undergraduate students each semester.

They notice when a tear forms in John's eye as he recounts his experiences. "Why didn't you just ask for help?" they ask each time, completely unaware that this is a collective, shame-based secret harbored by tens of thousands who have pegged themselves as defective, and so why would they ask? The universal desire to disappear from a literate society swarming with words grows.

Two polar opposite sets of experiences define my career:

The lived experiences that come from reading difficulty—children unable to read year after year; teachers desperately trying to teach their lowest performers; adults unable to work, participate in, or enrich their lives. These I call the "Something is Very Broken" experiences.

Scientific intervention studies highlighting large-scale, successful reading outcomes; my advisor, who involved me in research in which we successfully taught children how to read and teachers how to teach; and research scientists at annual conferences displaying data from successful experimental outcomes. These I call the "We Know What to Do!" experiences.

It is sickening, then, to witness failure to thrive in reading and to know that it is preventable. Why aren't we broadcasting to toddlers' parents the red flags that indicate potential future literacy problems? Why aren't reliable screenings to identify who needs intervention implemented consistently and properly? Why are highly effective interventions to both prevent and remediate reading difficulty summarily dismissed in favor of practices known to allow students' achievement to flatline?

Knowledge of evidence-based, highly effective reading practices must be prioritized, because all students *can* learn to read, and all educators *can* teach all students to read. I believe we must unite to share our expertise and experiences to motivate the appropriate remedies. We have this now in the The Reading League, a grassroots organization we created here in central New York dedicated to advancing the awareness, understanding, and use of evidence-based practices. None of us will ever know everything there is to know—but we owe it to the millions of little and big John and Jane Corcorans still out there to keep learning.

I will never forget a 24-year-old "John Corcoran" type student whom I tutored for five years. He had graduated from high school unable to read a single word. It had been assumed for 13 years of schooling that "he just isn't able to learn to read." Of course he could. During our second session, he successfully blended sounds together to read simple words and sentences. "Ten men had a van." He dabbed away tears of anger and disbelief, and faintly whispered, "I just read something." This is John Corcoran's *Literacy Manifesto*, and it is also a Declaration of Reading Independence for each of us who desires to make the inscrutable . . . scrutable.

# Foreword

*by Jose L. Cruz*

As I close in on 35 years of devoting my life's work to the current national literacy initiative, I long—still—for systemic changes that are yet to emerge after years of watching dedicated instruction, collaborations, and advocacy from diverse sources for our cause.

In my literacy career, I have had the honor of being a part of efforts that require large numbers of partners to engage in selfless collaboration. Like most people who work in literacy, I was drafted into this cause by surprise; off-script; not in the plan. I found myself in "special assignments" working for a statewide literacy coalition, a regional one, and one that has been my passion and employer for 25 years: The San Diego Council on Literacy. In addition, I am a member of the board of directors of ProLiteracy, the largest community-based literacy organization in the world.

While all of those roles are important to literacy, none is more important than that of the literacy student—something I am not.

In the latter part of the 1980s, I watched as adult literacy students across the country found the courage to tell their stories to powerful audiences everywhere, including elected officials in city halls, at state capitals, and in Washington, D.C.

In 1987, I was nearby when a new and exciting literacy story was breaking. A teacher from a local high school was considering going public with his secret. He had taught high school for 17 years and could not read above a second -grade level. Amazing.

In that year, I sat in the audience of the *Stanley Tonight* show with John Corcoran, who was also in the audience. I knew that he was there to see what happens when literacy students tell their stories. I watched John from a distance, hoping that what he saw would be enough to encourage him to take the next big step.

Months later, I saw John speak at the San Diego Council on Literacy's first and only *Business Breakfast for Literacy* with Jim Duffy from ABC-TV. Since then, John has been telling his story nonstop. Thirty years later, he is doing so with no less passion, no less fire, and no less enthusiasm.

In this book, John Corcoran's third, is contained the history of literacy, in the beginning and in modern times. He shares more of his story—testimonials through interludes, data, and other documentation—that helps us to understand the who, what, when, where, and why of illiteracy in America in a way that is compelling, engaging, emotional, and hopeful. Here, John has succeeded in packaging this cause in a way that will equip the average reader with everything anyone ever needed to know about this important skill and asset that affects all of us in everyday life.

Today we live in a world where people are easily distracted, where everyone can have their own website, blog, and Facebook page; where everyone carries their phone and camera everywhere to deliver photos and other messaging. The arrows are pointing in every direction—because everyone has an arrow.

Through the internet and technology, we have found ways to communicate more, but not to communicate *better*. It takes a lot to produce a document—in this case, a book—that succeeds in catching the eye, informing, entertaining, and laying the foundation for the kind of change that is vital to our democracy, to our quality of life, to individuals, families, and communities, and to employers who count on a skilled workforce of productive and competent workers.

With so much messaging, so much hype, and so many products and causes, it takes a special person—one who has been there, stayed there, collected information along the way while being there, and processed that information and accessed every part of his being—to state the truth about the problem and share solutions and vision, in a way that is inspiring and, yes, achievable.

It is imperative that we do more to work collaboratively, break down silos, and bring warranted attention to the short list of causes that affect all that we do. For good reasons, communicated here by John and partners, our elected officials, educators, corporate America, the media, moms, and dads, *everyone* needs to come together to fix this one important thing that is fixable that could do so much to affect a lot of other problems. By addressing literacy with family stability issues, it could be a whole new world.

John has captured all that we need to know to make lasting change happen. Now, with the clock ticking, he is inviting us to act. We just need to know enough, want enough, and believe as strongly as he does. He gives us every reason to do so, and for this, I am grateful. We should all be.

# Prologue: Sink or Swim

*In 1986, at the age of 48, I walked into a library in the next town and asked to see the head of the literacy program. After almost a half-century of fiercely guarding my story, the words poured out of me. I was a college graduate, I told her, a former high school teacher and founder of a multi-million-dollar real estate company. I was a husband and father and had almost everything a person could want in life. But I also had a secret I could no longer endure keeping. I did not know how to read.*

All stories begin with two things in common. The first is words, and the second is a human being who threads them together. My own life story began with a prolonged battle with words, an ongoing war from which I could never escape. I understood there was a struggle inside me long before I suspected it had a cause. A child of seven or eight is not likely to realize they have difficulties *because* they can't read. They will register only the difficulty itself, concluding that if they are constantly in trouble, they must be doing something wrong. A failing grade translates to a failing *person*—a bad student is bad, period. The cycle of educational crime and punishment takes on a life of its own, gradually gaining control of the child's identity. That is how it happened to me. I was at the mercy of a system that had unwittingly excluded me. I had passed through three grade levels in school, but I had not learned to read. I knew I was being punished, but I did not know what I had done wrong.

*Don't worry, he's a smart boy*, my parents were told. *He'll catch up*, my teachers promised. In hindsight, it is a remarkable attitude in its lack of logic. The ship of literacy had sailed, and I had been left behind at the dock. My classmates had moved on, heading somewhere new. Exactly how, I now wonder, did those teachers imagine I was going to *catch up?*

Some four decades later, my story took an unexpected turn. It started when I realized the cloak of pretense I had spent over 40 years patching together was slowly suffocating me. The change truly began when I threw the cloak off, asked for help, and found someone who could teach me how to read. The more I learned, the more I realized how powerless illiteracy had made me, no matter what I had accomplished in my life. I had come from a loving and supportive family and had always been given what I needed in life as a child, and I had always provided for myself and my family as an adult; and yet, I had spent most of my life without power. Without the skill of literacy, we are fundamentally disenfranchised.

The new learning-to-read chapter of my life brought me a great deal of attention, and with it, opportunity. Suddenly doors opened to me almost faster than I could walk through them. I appeared on national television shows and published a memoir called *The Teacher Who Couldn't Read*, was appointed to the advisory board of the National Institute for Literacy by President George H. W. Bush, and served under both Bush and President Clinton and continue to serve on the Board of the San Diego Council on Literacy. I testified at two congressional hearings on education and published a second book. I ate popcorn and watched a movie at the White House with President Clinton and his family, and I have spent the last 30 years speaking to audiences from all walks of life in the hopes of educating others about the consequences of failing to teach our children to read and write.

That failure is very real, and alarming. The current statistics are staggering. Our illiteracy/sub-literacy has not improved for more than a decade. It is estimated there are over 30,000,000 adults in this country who cannot read, and that 19% of all high school graduates are considered functionally illiterate. The role of illiteracy/sub-literacy in contributing to the poverty cycle, unemployment level, and the potential for incarceration is extreme. In my opinion, illiteracy/sub-literacy is one of America's most serious and insidious problems, and yet it is an issue that can be tackled effectively and inexpensively. Why then, are we failing?

I am not a scholar, a politician, or a Hollywood superstar. But I am uniquely qualified to be a whistle blower on behalf of all students who have difficulty learning, to be an advocate for educators who want to be better prepared to teach all students to read, and to be an activist for a revolution of learning. This book is my plea to readers, writers, and all lovers of learning and the written word to make literacy a priority.

Seventy years ago, I understood there were consequences to being left behind. I didn't know how or why I'd missed the boat, but I knew I had to take the plunge and struggle to try to keep my head above water, no matter what I had to do or say to survive. The stakes are simple, and they are high—the illiterate and sub-literate sink while the literate swim. I struggled against the tide for decades, barely keeping my head above the water, until finally, without the strength to continue the struggle, I asked for help.

I am asking for help again. This is my literacy manifesto.

# CHAPTER ONE

# A Brief History of Literacy

*B*y the third grade, I knew where I belonged. It was in the "dumb row", the classroom seats set aside for the slow, the rebellious, and the short-sighted. In the dumb row, we were separated from the regular kids, clustered together for no common reason other than our poor academic standing. The reason for relegating us to our own territory is unclear, since denizens of the dumb row were neither given different academic consideration nor immune from the punishment visited upon those unwilling or unable to read what was written on the blackboard. Day after day, I accepted demerits or rapped calves and knuckles for what I could not fake my way out of. I never questioned the fairness of the system. It was clear enough. The dumb row was there to put me in my place, and keep me there.

The history of literacy is complicated, but it has always been connected to power. When we talk about "literate" in today's terms, it is a quality that is understood as something positive and beneficial. At the same time, it is a presumed standard of what we consider normal and necessary in our society. It is interesting that while the word "illiteracy" has been in use for over 350 years, the word "literacy" doesn't appear in the English language until 1880, when it was first used in an American periodical. The quality of being educated in letters was so specific and limited, no word was needed in our language to describe it.

Certainly, for many centuries the skills of reading and writing were mostly limited to the rich or powerful, or those who worked on their behalf. In part, this is common sense. An ordinary pre-15th century individual had neither the means nor the justification to learn a skill that did not help put food on the table. But in a larger sense, keeping the masses sub-literate was an important way for an elite few to control knowledge and communication and maintain their own power. But in 1540, an ingenious invention changed all that. The printing press proved to be the force that opened the Pandora's box of literacy.

The invention of the printing press made it possible to produce books in quantity, instead of one at a time copied in longhand.

The invention did not change the fact that few people were able to read printed material. It is believed only a small fraction of Europe's population could read when Gutenberg put the finishing touches on his moveable type press. But books, pamphlets, and newspapers offered a dangerous opportunity for spreading ideas opposing the status quo. As an example of how widespread the concern was, Pope Alexander VI declared that anyone printing texts not approved by the Catholic Church would be excommunicated.

But the tide of progress couldn't be turned—the printing press was here to stay. The Church began to lose its hold over the practice of Christianity itself. The sacred texts and liturgies had long been available only in handwritten copies laboriously created by monks and scribes. The resulting manuscripts were exquisite and valuable works of art, but not easily obtained—and not easy to read. Like the Catholic liturgy itself, they were written in Latin, a language understood only by a slim percentage of scholars and clergy. The Church therefore enjoyed a position as the sole and necessary interpreter of all sacred texts and liturgies. Congregants could only understand the texts as interpreted by the clergy. They could not understand the services they attended, as they were conducted in a language they did not understand. The clergy remained the necessary middlemen, without whom the ordinary person could not navigate the precarious path between salvation and damnation. As long as the masses were dependent on the clergy to translate the word of God, they could be controlled by their desire to be upstanding members of the Catholic community.

It's not surprising, that to translate the Bible into English was decreed a criminal act punishable by death. It isn't surprising that even the power of the Roman Catholic Church couldn't prevent such translations from happening. William Tyndale is thought to be the first to print and publish an English translation of the New Testament. For that act he was burned at the stake, but the damage to the Church's authority and the Protestant reforms set in place by Martin Luther and others meant that for the first time the common man had direct access to holy scripture. With it, he gained control over his life and his soul.

**The Puritan belief in the importance of Bible reading meant that education was considered a priority.**

When the first colonies were established in North America in the early 1600s, the Puritan belief in the importance of Bible reading meant that education was considered a priority. The responsibility lay at home with individual families, but was also addressed in the law as a component in becoming a law-abiding and productive member of society. A 1642 Massachusetts law stated that "all youth under family Government shall be taught to read perfectly the English tongue, have knowledge in capital laws, and be taught some orthodox catechisms, and that they be brought up to some honest employment, profitable to themselves, and to the Commonwealth."

By the 18th century, the importance of literacy had been embraced by the founding fathers of America. Thomas Jefferson proposed a bill to create free public schools that would teach reading, writing, and math to "all the free children, male and female." Jefferson's careful and limiting choice of the words "free children" give a clear picture of the importance at the time of keeping American slaves illiterate.

In a country founded on freedom and the understanding in Thomas Jefferson's words in a letter to Virginia legislator Charles Yancey that "Where the press is free, and every man able to read, all is safe," literacy once again became an important element of control. Knowledge—and the ability to be effective communicators of thoughts and ideas through the written word—was power. Some states, to counter and prevent the formation of this power, passed laws prohibiting the teaching of reading or writing to any slave. In 1870, five years after the Civil War that ended the practice of slavery, the word "literacy" made its first known appearance in the American lexicon.

The road from the end of slavery to the beginning of real educational opportunities for African-Americans was long and bleak, as the nation assumed a longstanding indifference. In the first years of Reconstruction, volunteer teachers streamed into the South and hundreds of schools were built and supplied by northern aid organizations. The literacy movement flourished. This focused not just on children but on the many adult African-Americans who were desperate to obtain the education they were now entitled as freedmen to receive. In some private homes throughout the South, family members taught literacy skills to their African-American servants in secret because literate African-Americans were seen as a threat.

But the momentum sparked powerful resistance and could not sustain itself beyond several decades of Jim Crow laws and other legal restrictions designed to limit the freedom and opportunities of African-Americans. It wasn't until the 1950s that the United States and the federal government began a committed push to address the problem, beginning with the Supreme Court decision in *Brown v. Board of Education* which declared the legally-sanctioned state concept of "separate but equal" unconstitutional.

Census data taken in the United States in 1870 shows that 1 out of 5 people of all races over the age of fourteen could not read or write in any language. The number of non-literate people dropped steadily for the next hundred years. However, findings from the National Center for Educational Statistics (NCES) has found that between 1992 and 2003, the level of adult literacy levels defined as "below basic" (no more than the most simple and concrete skills) had no marked improvement. The NCES data indicates that people with below basic or sub-literate levels in 2003 for prose literacy comprised 14% of the population, or roughly 30 million people. The number of those categorized as having only "basic" skills—defined as being able to perform only simple or everyday literacy activities—was 29%, or some 63 million adults.

**According to more recent findings from the U.S. Department of Education and the National Institute of Literacy in a 2016 survey, the percentage of adult Americans who cannot read above a basic level has remained at 14% since 2003.**

According to more recent findings from the U.S. Department of Education and the National Institute of Literacy in a 2016 survey, the percentage of adult Americans who cannot read above a basic level has remained at 14% since 2003. In other words, there has been absolutely no improvement. An alarming number of Americans are not being taught the literacy skills they need to function and flourish in the world.

Always a double-edged sword, the very subject of literacy itself has become weaponized. Some current books and essays on the subject cast illiteracy/sub-literacy as the symptom of a systematic conspiracy launched by a group, political party, or presidential administration with the intent of dumbing down an entire generation of schoolchildren. Laying blame and inventing a cause for the epidemic of illiteracy/sub-literacy in America contributes absolutely nothing to improving the situation. Is it any wonder that educators are increasingly defensive, and that the statistics around literacy fail to improve?

In short, there must be more proacitivity—not just from government but from community organizations, including those based in faith. In Pope John Paul II's 1995 "Message for Lent" he described illiteracy as a "hidden sickness" and made reference to Pope Paul VI's famous observation that "lack of education is as serious as lack of food; the illiterate person is a starved spirit."

The Pope's 1995 message urged that proactive movement be taken to address this hidden sickness. He wrote, "Faced with the seriousness of the living conditions of our brothers and sisters who are kept at a distance from modern culture, we have a duty to show them our complete solidarity. Actions undertaken to favor access to reading and writing are the first condition for helping the impoverished to mature intellectually and to lead their lives more independently. Literacy and education are an essential duty and investment for humanity's future, for 'the fulfillment of the whole man and of every man', as Paul VI said."

These calls to action must be heeded. Institutions don't change themselves; people change them from the outside, and this is a plea for individuals to prioritize and implement those changes wherever they have influence, whether in government, churches, grassroots organizations, or simply starting in their own homes.

The reality is that with a basic understanding of the history, science, and educational forces at work behind literacy, multiple levels of affordable and accessible solutions become clear. While it may be tempting for some to remain in the arena of blame, those who truly wish to help have many resources open to them.

In order to better identify where those opportunities lie, we must first understand where the obstacles and the gatekeepers are to be found.

# INTERLUDE: "A WRITER ON READING" BY T. R. HUMMER

I was seven years old when I was possessed by texts—by writing: when speech took a back seat to reading in a deep way in my mind and I began to think not in utterance, but in prose.

I was an early reader, finding my way from picture books to comic books to novels between the ages of four and five. I had a hunger for stories, and though I lived in the deep South, where storytelling is supposed to be ubiquitous, no one ever told me any, so books had to serve.

At the library, I turned up at the help desk, barely tall enough to see over it.

"Can I help you?" the librarian asked.

"Do you have *The Jungle Book* by Ru-yard Kipling?" I asked.

She blinked. "Rudyard," she said. "Yes, of course."

Once I had begun, I read constantly, night and day. In those days, before computers and—in our house—before television, my parents would often say "You spend too much time reading; you should go play outside." (Now, of course, the admonition is "You spend too much time staring at a screen; you should read a book.")

The summer I was seven, I discovered Zane Grey, whose work occupied me for six months or so. I was reading one of his novels when my mother told me, "It's time for lunch; put away your book."

"Okay." I said, but my inner voice began replaying the dialog: *It's time for lunch, she said,* I heard, and then, *Okay, he answered.* Our real voices replayed in my head as prose, as dialog from a novel, and once that process started I could not make it stop. It went on for days, for weeks, any time I or anyone spoke.

Clean your room. *"Clean your room," she said.* In a minute. *"In a minute," he answered.*

Everything happened twice. It was a tic, or perhaps a compulsion. I had no control over it. It was a kind of bliss, a kind of torture, and perhaps, in the end, a kind of power to be a character in the book of my own life.

# CHAPTER TWO

# The Gatekeepers

*T**here was no "dumb row" in my new school in Los Alamos, New Mexico, but I soon learned I didn't need one. In Los Alamos, I was punished not with the stinging slaps of a yardstick on my legs but with something that caused a deeper, more damaging kind of pain. I was ignored. The first time my fourth-grade teacher asked me to read aloud and I could not, she did not ask me what the matter was. She did not take me aside after class to privately investigate why I had not responded. Instead, as my classmates snickered, she said, "Cat got your tongue?" When I was still unable to answer, she sighed, and I could see the resignation cross her face. Oh, he's one of those—another stupid one. With that unspoken dismissal, she turned her attention to a student who could answer, and that was that. No demerits, no welts on my legs. This teacher punished me with silence. I had been tried and convicted of stupidity, and my punishment was to be ignored.*

*Now I understood why my new school had no need for a "dumb row." They had a better way to deal with me. They simply ignored me. They let me know through their silence that I was not a student.*

*I was not a person.*

*I was nobody.*

In 1963, less than ten years after the announcement that a new vaccine was proving up to 90% effective against paralytic polio, a new epidemic was identified—one that millions of school children were at risk of being diagnosed with. The epidemic came with an array of symptoms, but no identifiable origin or cause. There was no cure. Once teachers went on the alert for this insidious and incurable disease, it appeared to be spreading rapidly through-out the national school system. Those who had it were unable to do some of the things that their classmates seemed to do with virtually no effort. The name given to those suffering from this debilitating condition was "learning-disabled."

To understand where we went wrong in establishing this diagno-sis, it is important to have a general understanding of the history and intention of special education laws, created to protect a seg-ment of the student population deemed to be at risk for a reduced access to education. As far back as the late 19th century, some states created laws to reduce or eliminate delinquency, geared toward poverty-stricken students and those residing in urban slums who were more likely than their better-off counterparts to miss school.

Other laws addressed the issues of child labor, limiting hours and prohibiting the employment of any child who could not read or write unless they were able to attend night school. Nineteenth century schools for children with physical disabilities did exist, but most were private institutions, and laws governing them var-ied from state to state. Readers of Laura Ingalls Wilder's classic *Little House* children's book series are familiar with the plight of Mary Ingalls, who lost her sight to scarlet fever in 1879 at the age of fourteen. During that time, the territory of Dakota entered into a five-year contract with the Iowa College for the Blind and paid for eight years of Mary's education there. But many children with similar disabilities had no access to an institution like this, or could not afford uncovered costs.

In the 20th century, a series of landmark laws came into effect addressing the needs of students who were unable to obtain an adequate education. The landmark Supreme Court decision of 1954, *Brown v. Board of Education*, ruled that segregation of chil-dren in public schools deprived those children of the equal edu-cational opportunities to which they were entitled. In the 1972

*Mills v. Board of Education of the District of Columbia,* the Supreme Court found that schools excluding disabled children from attendance were violating the right of all children to a free public education. In the congressional investigation that followed, it was determined that, in fact, 2.5 million children with physical or mental handicaps were receiving either an inadequate education or no education at all. In 1975, a new public law came into effect to address that alarming shortfall.

**In the early 1970s it was determined that 2.5 million children with physical or mental handicaps were receiving either inadequate or no education at all.**

The new law, Public Law 94-142, made a profound change in the lives of countless disabled students and their families. It is undeniable that the outcome of this law, also called the Education for All Handicapped Children Act (and, more recently, the Individuals with Disabilities Education Act) was overwhelmingly positive. Congress demonstrated that even beyond the issue of equity, the exclusion of disabled children from education benefits came at a devastating cost. The committee report included the finding that "public agencies and taxpayers will spend billions of dollars over the lifetimes of these individuals to maintain such persons as dependents and in a minimally acceptable lifestyle. With proper education services, many would be able to become productive citizens contributing to society instead of being forced to remain burdens. Others, through such services, would increase their independence, thus reducing their dependence on society." The law made it mandatory for public schools to accommodate and serve children with mental or physical handicaps. Eventually the word "disability" was used in place of the word "handicap."

How did the very helpful educational Public Law 94-142 result in the creation of an umbrella diagnosis for struggling learners that did more damage than good? The problem, in hindsight, is easy to identify. The special education model was very successful for children with actual physical or mental handicaps. However, it was not an accurate model for categorizing or addressing the needs of the non-handicapped students who have difficulty learning in a traditional classroom—those who used to be called "slow to learn." An individual's struggle to learn is not a physical disability as we understand it—is not a handicap, or even a fixed condition. It does not require different physical accommodations, such as wheelchair ramps, sound amplification, or large print; but the label "learning disabled" belies this. The moment we accepted that label into our lexicon, we sabotaged our fundamental ability to understand, legislate, and prepare our teachers to effectively assist non-handicapped students—children who had normal intelligence and were called "slow to learn", but in reality simply needed to be taught in a way that made sense to them.

Some experts in the field believe that the existence of a one-size-fits-all diagnosis of "learning disabled" is not only a basic mis-identification, but it is also a model that places the blame of failure to learn on the students themselves. The vague label of "learning disabled" gave birth to a vast array of research into that same syndrome, as if it were a biologically based illness or condition. The result of that research was the expansion of a smaller set of labels that are just as vague: dyslexia, script blindness, attention deficit disorder, and word amblyopia. Research indicates that the very tests designed to diagnose learning disabilities are ineffective, and yet researchers have been reluctant to stop creating studies designed to support the theory that learning disabilities are caused by biologically-based disorders in the brain.

In other words, the foundation of the "learning disability" diagnosis was built on sand, yet we continue to add layers to the structure while ignoring evidence of its instability. In spite of overwhelming evidence to the contrary, the education community has continued to cling to the medical model blueprint of "learning disability", and to the pseudo-science that supports it. And why not? An enormous industry has sprung from it, and where there is industry there is money. The medical model encourages research, targeted programs, and cost-efficient classroom solutions, all while implicitly reinforcing that our teachers, educators, parents, and public-school system itself are as blameless for the outbreak as they were in the epidemic of polio.

This sense of blamelessness is both convenient and a fatally flawed truth, and as long as we continue to cling to it, some children will continue falling behind in school. We are in a position now to prove that failure to learn is *not* a biological condition rooted in a structural flaw in the brain. This is not merely an option—it is an imperative.

The controversy over the model of "learning disability" is a heated one, and in fairness, the resistance of the educational community is understandable. The foundation of the current model is now over a half-century old, and in those 50 years, level after level of policy and process have been built atop it.

To dismantle that system would be a massive undertaking involving changing every level of the system, from the classroom to the way that teachers themselves are instructed to approach learning. In his book *Language at the Speed of Sight,* Mark Seidenberg writes, "Teaching requires a professional model, like we have in medicine, law, engineering, accounting, architecture, and many other fields. In these professions, consistency of quality is created less by holding individual practitioners accountable and more by building a body of knowledge, carefully training people in that knowledge, requiring them to show expertise before they become licensed, and then using their professions' standards to guide their work. By these criteria, American education is a failed profession."

Though created with the best of intentions, the very label of "learning disabled" itself is both inaccurate and disenfranchising. We have explored the ways in which tapping into the disability culture established a blame-free explanation for the growing number of students falling behind in school. We have also identified the motivation for persisting—an industry has been created to support this disability myth, and that industry attracts money.

There is one final and crucial component to understand if we are to find our way out of the quicksand. We have inadvertently created a concentrated source of power and control over the millions of students who fall under any of the many categories collected under the "learning disability" umbrella. That power source is made up of the individuals driving and profiting from the learning disability industry. They are the people behind the endless programs and policies and protocols, and those people are the gatekeepers of literacy. Unable or unwilling to concede that their model has been built on a fundamentally flawed model, those gatekeepers guard the road to literacy and clutter it with so many detours and roadblocks that it has become hopelessly impassable. The students' experience does not change because the teachers' methodology has not been updated and standardized.

Seidenberg writes, "Parents who deliver their children to school on that momentous first day of kindergarten proudly starting them on the venerable path to education make a big mistake: they assume that their child's teacher has been taught how to teach reading. They haven't." The under-preparation of teachers is one of the most significant obstacles on an educational road already choked with blockages.

There is only one solution remaining: We must build a bridge over that road. We must bypass the gatekeepers and find another way to literacy altogether.

# INTERLUDE: "GRANDMA'S BOOKSHELF" BY ALEXA

My grandma was my safe place. I could count on her being there when I called on her, and I called on her often. She was a refuge in the midst of a childhood overshadowed by the chaos of my parents' addictions. My grandma loved to read; she loved books and she passed on her love for reading and books to me early in life. She owned a small bookstore called the Bookshelf, where I spent many hours tucked quietly in a carpeted aisle lined with books, feeling safe and loved and able to escape into an imaginary world found in the words of stories. Reading came very easily to me. If it hadn't, I can't imagine how much more difficult life would have been.

The book *The Secret Garden* had a significant impact on me. I saw myself in each of the characters. Mary's parents were not there, so she spent much of her time alone; she was selfish, demanding, and self-absorbed, without the necessary discipline and parenting to know otherwise. Colin's friendships and the fruit of his hard work gave him hope that he would survive his devastating circumstances and that he might even thrive. These characters showed me how fun it could be to find solace in nature, and how friends can become the family we choose when our own family doesn't resemble what we see around us. Reading gave me a perspective that lessened the fear in my real life and gave me companions in my difficult circumstances. Reading introduced me to new ideas and new possibilities.

As a child, I remember feeling as if the people who were supposed to be there for me had been taken captive. I often felt powerless. Perhaps this is why I was captivated by the *Choose Your Own Adventure* books that were amongst my favorite stories. Reading these books helped me to begin to learn the power of my own choices and the importance of considering multiple possible outcomes.

In these books, the reader is on a journey as the main character and arrives at a crossroads. Once at the crossroads, a choice must be made to move ahead in the story. Whatever choice is made sends the reader to another section of the book. If the reader chooses to fight the enemy, for example, they turn to page 9. If they tuck their tail and run, they go to page 17. Often times during that season of my life, I felt just the same as when I was at the crossroads in one of those books, and I was choosing the lesser of two evils. At that young age I couldn't articulate what I was learning, yet in hindsight I can see how those stories helped me to grasp the freedom and power of my own choices.

Even though my grandmother endured much grief in her life, including the tragic sudden loss of her firstborn son in a car accident and her firstborn daughter living with the devastation of addiction, she never lost her faith in God. She often reminded me to pray, and that God heard my prayers, and to keep talking to Him, and she consistently said, "Here, go read a book." The most influential book I have ever read is the Bible. My grandma was not a traditionally religious woman, but her faith in God was unshaken even as she took her last breath. Reading this love letter from God through the Bible continues to give me wisdom and hope. It's no surprise then that when my grandma was in her final hours, the one thing I could think of to comfort her was to read the Bible, this love letter, to her. Here I was, an adult, sharing with her the gift she had given to me, reading to her about our perfect refuge. I am forever grateful for my grandma, my childhood refuge, and for her sharing her love of reading with me.

# The Reading Brain

*F*ifth-grade. New school. New kids. New teachers. Old labels. School was a battlefield. Outside the classroom, I soon became a target of bullying. Nowhere was safe. I was under siege. I had to learn fast how to defend myself. When to push back. When to bluff. In self-defense, I created a persona. A false self, becoming someone I wasn't—Loco Johnny. Crazy Johnny. To my amazement, people believed it.

*Inside the classroom, I soon became a target of familiar labels.*

- ☑ Lacks motivation
- ☑ Displays immaturity
- ☑ Unresponsive to classwork

*Nowhere was safe. I was under siege. I had to learn fast.*

*But I couldn't.*

*In self-defense, I created a persona. A false self. Becoming someone I wasn't.*

*Reading Johnny. Literate Johnny.*

*Again, to my amazement, people believed it.*

What is reading? What exactly happens in the brain so a series of written letters or words are translated into thought and understanding? The written word is a code for a spoken or oral form of language, so we can look at reading as the process of breaking that code. The key to unlocking the code can only be found in physical study of the human brain itself.

> **Neuroscientists have concluded that the human brain is not designed to accommodate the process of reading.**

In the last several decades, neuroscientists have made enormous advances in understanding the incredibly complex task of reading. The evidence now shows that the original presumptions educators and specialists used to diagnose and treat the failure to learn were based on inaccurate or incomplete information. To understand how and why we got off course on the road to literacy, we need look no farther than the findings of neuroscience.

Before the arrival of neuroimaging technology like MRI, there was no way to simply look into a brain to find out how it functioned. Creating hypotheses and diagnoses from a vague symptom such as "slow learner" was a shaky process at best, but for a time, no significant alternative existed. Imagine trying to figure out how a television worked only by watching TV programs, and never taking the device apart to look inside. Actually, looking inside a television set would only introduce more confusion. The usual/best way to learn how television works is to "read" about them—that way you could understand them even if you never saw one.

Reliance on indirect evidence to understand the process of reading is no longer necessary now that devices like MRI and fMRI give us a direct look inside the working brain. Incredibly, scientists can now document the entire reading process, from the moment the eye registers letters to the explosion of connections made out through sound, vision, and memory—all happening in a split second. With the means to observe and compare the brains of adults with infants, and of readers with non-readers, neuroscientists such as Stanislas Dehaene have concluded that the human brain was not designed to accommodate the process of reading.

When we consider that the invention of alphabets occurred just a few thousand years ago, and that as recently as the Middle Ages most humans never even tried learning to read, this design flaw becomes more understandable.

For the brain to master an ability so outside its original capabilities requires a remarkable feat—what amounts to a significant rewiring of some of its circuitry. And though this arduous neuro-adaptation is not passed down to our offspring, the capacity to do it is. In generation after generation, the brains of young children reroute countless neural pathways so that written language can be navigated. And what do we call that complex neural redesign that fundamentally changes what the brain is able to do? We call it "learning to read," and we expect children to take to it intuitively, though it is anything but natural or simple.

That rearrangement of neural pathways takes place without our direct knowledge, as the process will take care of itself if the proper conditions are presented. So in spite of certain cognitive limitations based on its design, the brain is remarkably adaptive. Its ability to change itself based on physical needs or behavior is called neuroplasticity. With the help of neuroimaging, we have learned that the brains of musicians look different from those of non-musicians, and that people who have meditated for many years leave a visible change in their cerebral structure. It is scientifically evident that we can change our brains through certain behaviors or methods of learning. Neuroplasticity also plays a role in physical health; the brain can work to repair physical damage to neural cells. After suffering a stroke in which cells in the speech or memory center are damaged, for example, the brain can be rewired through training to compensate for what has been lost. In the process of this rewiring, the brain can essentially build a detour around a damaged area. It can even grow new neurons to replace the damaged ones.

For generations, the accepted scientific model of reading was fairly simple and linear—the retina perceived a word, and the signal passed through various centers in the brain to pick up the visual, auditory, and contextual data that allow that word to be understood. But today, when brain activity is mapped in real-time, scientists can actually observe what happens during the process of reading. We now know that the system is infinitely more complicated than once imagined, and that information is split into pieces and transmitted to many parts of the brain before a word can be decoded or understood.

How do these advances in neuroscience help us to understand how and where we took a wrong turn on the path to literacy? To begin with, our relatively new access to a biological map of the reading brain enables us to see some things we were *wrong* about: Reading ability is an acquired skill, *not* a fixed function of IQ.

All human brains must adapt in order to accommodate reading—children are *not* born with an innate inclination to learn to read as naturally as they learn to speak.

No two brains are alike, and therefore the way the brain adapts to accommodate reading will *not* be the same in every person. Individual difficulty with learning is *not* a disability.

Cognitive neurologist Martha Bridge Denckla has said, referring to our long attachment to labels like dyslexia, that "we need to be thinking of it as a variant of normal, rather than an abnormality." What reasons exists for her position? Largely, it stems from better scientific understanding. Previously the approach to so-called slow learners involved a great deal of guesswork and the ad hoc nature of the medical disability model. Now that the contradictory evidence is so overwhelming, it would seem natural that educators would be quick to update the model so that teachers would be better trained to help all students learn to read. But that isn't what happened.

**In most states today, whole language reading continues to be embraced in spite of the growing evidence of its fallibility.**

Clearly our educational system has failed to keep pace with current knowledge. By some accounts the entire approach has been backwards, and too much time and energy is spent trying to define something that isn't easily definable. As Stanislas Dehaene wrote in *Reading in the Brain*, neuroscience has demonstrated that "to define what reading is *not* is a good starting point. As over-trained readers, we no longer have much perspective on how difficult reading really is. We tend to believe that one glance at a word will transfer its immediate and global identification in a single step. Nothing could be further from the truth."

Dehaene cites a glaring example of this in the approach to literacy called "whole language." In short, it is a model of teaching literacy skills that focuses on a learned recognition of sentences without the letter-by-letter decoding or sounding out of individual words. A significant conflict grew between proponents of whole language learning and those structured around phonics (sounding out the letters in a word). The whole language movement began in the early 1950s, before most of the scientific findings discussed in this chapter had occurred. But today, in most states, whole language thinking continues to be embraced and stressed in textbooks in spite of growing evidence that neuroscience has refuted its core presumption.

California was a state that enthusiastically supported and promoted whole language learning and adopted whole-language textbooks. There was strong opposition from parents and from professionals like researcher and neuroscientist G. Reid Lyon, who had numerous studies finding students had a better learning rate with phonics than with whole language. Nonetheless, policymakers clung to whole language more stubbornly than ever. In 1990, the National Assessment of Educational Progress ranked California's reading proficiency as the second worst in the country. Test scores reinforced the understanding provided by neuroscience—that the wiring of the brain, and the re-wiring that occurs when we learn to read—relied on the element of sound, or phonemes.

Hard, reputable scientific evidence failed to sway the policymakers of California's education system, but plummeting test scores could not be ignored. The cycle of failure to teach had dangerously intensified. Somehow, parents—and students themselves—had been elbowed out of their partnership with schools and teachers. It is now imperative educators identify neuroscience-supported teaching solutions, beginning with the acceptance that reading is a skill that some will pick up more quickly than others, just like musicality or athleticism. If we have a healthy student who cannot run well or touch his toes without extra effort or instruction, we don't assume he is athletics-disabled. We accept that some people have less physical prowess than others, or less muscle tissue, or poorer coordination. They are not disabled, they simply have a lower natural capacity for, say, basketball.

So how can understanding our capacity for neuroplasticity help us find specific solutions for the many students who don't thrive in a one-size-fits-all learning environment? We return to the science of reading. First, the eyes project images containing the words to be read onto the retinas which convert the patterns of light into action potentials which the optic nerves send on for complex processing in specialized areas of the cortex. Knowledge of these processes are providing important clues in how teaching reading can be most efficiently achieved for each and every student. We know that the component of sound and the creation of a string of sounds that make a word is a crucial factor. We also know that the process is not innately intuitional the way learning to speak *is*, and is therefore not something we just need to nudge to make it self-activate. For every question about reading and the teaching of reading, we now have a wealth of answers thanks to neuroscientific advances; and yet our educational system has proved remarkably stubborn to change in response to these discoveries. This "stubbornness" cannot be due to simple ignorance because the massive failure of the "whole language method" with millions of students is so obvious. It is crucial to understand the real motivation for this intentional dumbing down of our students (future citizens) by sabotaging their abilities to read.

G. Reid Lyon has written that "despite strong evidence to the contrary, many educators and researchers maintain the perspective that reading is an almost instinctive, natural process. They believe that explicit instruction in phoneme awareness, phonics, structural analysis, and reading comprehension strategies is unnecessary because oral language skills provide the reader with a meaning-based structure for the decoding and recognition of unfamiliar words." So, the question remains: When science has provided a map to the treasure of literacy, why are educators and policymakers continuing to dig in the wrong place?

This *Literacy Manifesto* is intended to identify what *must* change in our perception and educational approach so that teachers are better equipped to respond to what students need. It becomes unacceptable for one out of every five students to fall behind in the classroom. Top on that list of changing perception and approach is paying attention to the true science, and dispensing with the pseudoscience. Paula and Keith Stanovich, in their Partnership for Reading paper "Using Research and Reason in Education," summed it up nicely. They wrote, "As professionals, teachers can become more effective and powerful by developing the skills to recognize scientifically based practice and, when the evidence is not available, use some basic research concepts to draw conclusions on their own." In the paper's conclusion, they write, "Researchers and educators are kindred spirits in their approach to knowledge, an important fact that can be used to forge a coalition to bring hard-won research knowledge to light in the classroom."

In the kind of environment Paula and Keith Stanovich describe, the student could resume his or her rightful place as the most important person in the classroom.

# CHAPTER FOUR

# The Disabling Label

*B*y the sixth grade, the growing gap between my classmates and I began to harden me. Bewildered as to why this was happening, I continued to encounter teachers who treated me as if I were stupid. I knew only two things resolutely: that I was not stupid, and that teachers' unfair relegation of me as hopeless was beginning to take its toll.

*If my oppressors insisted on seeing me as the stubborn rebel, then I decided that was exactly what I would become. I befriended others who had been relegated to similar cubbyholes, and crafted a new version of myself. I was the tough guy, the wisecracker, the trouble-maker. I was the one who just didn't care.*

*I donned this mask each morning on arriving at school, and took it off every afternoon before returning home. Finally, I had seized upon a coping mechanism that would see me through the next several decades. I knew what skills worked, and I had them in spades. I cultivated them tirelessly, honing and refining them. At long last, I knew who I needed to be, and I turned myself into him.*

*I became an impostor.*

As children, we are taught that "sticks and stones may break my bones, but words will never hurt me." Such sayings are intended to comfort us and make us feel safe, sometimes by teaching a platitude that is a clear departure from reality. In truth, words most certainly can and do hurt, and can also be charged with an undeniable life and power of their own.

I come from the unique position of being a literacy advocate with four decades of experience being on the other side of the equation—unable to read. Today, we use "learning disability" as a conventional term. It was first coined in 1963 when Dr. Samuel Kirk, professor of special education at the University of Illinois, suggested its use to describe "children who had disorders in development of language, speech, reading, and associated communication skills."

**Teachers have inherited a flawed system and are routinely blamed for its educational shortcomings.**

I never attached the "learning disabled" label to myself, but I'm painfully familiar with its damaging effects and its ability to stigmatize, separate, and shame. In an era in which we have come to recognize the power of certain highly charged words and labels, I cannot help but consider this a basic issue of civil and human rights. For this reason, it is confounding that people of good intentions continue to label children with this language.

This is a manifesto, a call to action, and as such it does not benefit from placing blame. But it is important to understand what mistakes have been made—and how and why we made them—in order to move forward. Our teachers have inherited a flawed system and are often scapegoated for its shortcomings. That scapegoating should never have happened, but it is fallout from our reliance on classifications and special language and sub-debates, all of which only serve to get people out of the conversation.

Our goal is to widen the circle by focusing on what could be coined a "teaching disability", but is in actuality a shortfall in which teachers have not been taught what they need to know to most effectively teach reading. As national education expert

Louisa Moats said in her testimony before the House Committee on Education and the Workforce, "Teacher preparation in reading will require a systematic overhaul to reach every part of the problem . . . Only systematic rebuilding is likely to establish a profession that is informed by science, a profession that will meet every child's needs for reading success."

There seems little doubt that this is what all of us want, and the dire straits we currently find ourselves in are not due to lack of effort at a local or national level. The 2001 No Child Left Behind (NCLB) Act made important strides by spotlighting the gap between what our students should be capable of and where they actually stand. But at the same time, NCLB was dogged by problems from the beginning, including teacher resistance, especially to the act's accountability aspect. In addition, the NCLB Act was ultimately drawn into the political arena and was not reauthorized.

The problem-solving nature of the human brain brings with it a deep-seated inclination to attack a problem in steps that rationalize and then provide release. One of the earliest of those steps is the impetus to devise a name or label for a problem. It can, in fact, be helpful to take something intangible and reduce it to a recognizable word or name, organizing the incomprehensible into a diagram of smaller components—facilitating the mind into seeing the problem as tangible, and therefore beginning the process of reverse-engineering a solution.

But the opposite can sometimes hold true: The naming or labeling of a thing can halt that same cognitive process. Having named it, the mind is given a false sense of comfort and becomes complacent, releasing the problem altogether. The label itself, intended to facilitate solutions, instead becomes a perpetuating factor in the problem. One of the starkest examples of this has been the effect of the creation and adoption into our lexicon of the label "learning disabled."

As explored in an earlier chapter, the 1990 Individuals with Disabilities Education Act (IDEA) replaced older legislation and replaced the term "handicap" with "disability." This lateral step of exchanging one label for another deemed more politically correct provided nothing in the way of clarity of definition. It told us nothing about the who or the why of literacy ability. To this day, the label remains a mere designation of any number of cognitive processes related to speech, aural clarity, reading skills and comprehension, and reasoning.

With such vague definitional parameters, is it any wonder we have yet to establish a diagnostic tool, let alone implement an effective educational approach that actually addresses the issue? As G. Reid Lyon writes in *The Future of Children* this reliance on a hopelessly vague definition, coupled with the fact that the assessment of who falls into this category varies greatly from school to school, has resulted in an ominous "discrepancy standard." Never clear on what "learning disabled" actually meant in the first place, we are equally unclear how to test for it. This fundamental discordance, Lyon believes, "clearly promotes a wait-to-fail policy because a significant discrepancy between IQ and achievement generally cannot be detected until about eight or nine.

In fact, there are many school districts which do not identify children with learning disabilities until a child is reading well below grade level, generally in the third or fourth-grade. By this time, the child has already experienced at least a few years of school failure and probably has experienced the common attendant problems of low self-esteem, diminished motivation, and

**43% of Americans still incorrectly believe that learning disabilities are associated with low IQ!**

inadequate acquisition of the academic material covered by his classmates during the previous few years." In this way, the label of "learning disabled" has become a self-fulfilling prophecy that seeks out and creates the very characteristics in students that it purports to be merely identifying.

In the ultimate irony, this labeling serves to retroactively disable students, sabotaging their self-esteem and sequestering them without providing the understanding or tools to help them. We've dispensed with the dunce cap and the "dumb row" as cruel and uselessly stigmatizing, and yet, in an attempt to remedy that, we've created a more insidious form of stigmatization that masquerades as something both compassionate and effective. Forty-three percent of Americans still incorrectly believe that learning disabilities are associated with a low IQ. As a consequence of our reliance on a learning-disabled industry built on a foundation with no solid underpinning, we have become increasingly invested in labeling children and have institutionalized illiteracy and sub-literacy in a way that serves only that institution.

It has been more than a half-century since we have been using the term "learning disability." In that time, the field of special education has become a force to be reckoned with. By the late 1960s, many parents became more assertive in their desire to see schools do more for, and better by, their children. Once the "learning disabled" label caught on, a virtually endless array of tests and services sprang up to meet the needs of the ever-expanding population of students assessed as LD. While no single cause can ever be identified, it is obvious that one factor responsible for giving the special education business such steam is that the LD label removed any semblance of blame from either the parents or the educators. It is understandably human to put stock in the offered diagnosis that has no blame attached—that a cancer was caused by a fluke, for example, rather than by a chosen behavior such as smoking or drinking. The concept of LD took the onus of action off of parents and teachers and placed it into the custom-made structure of special education. Relieved of the burden of fault, educators and parents took comfort from the steady stream of money funding the new structure—everything will be okay, because something is *being done*. The resulting explosion of growth saw the special education industry take on a life of its own. Over time its primary function became to preserve and grow *itself* at the expense of the very people it was supposedly designed to help—students.

By all realistic accounts, we are woefully disserving our students, and revamping not just an educational system, but a deep-seated mindset, which is not something that can happen overnight. Making a change of this magnitude, as it has been described, is "like a battleship—it takes time to turn around." But there is one change we could make instantaneously without funding or fanfare. We could agree to quit using the "learning disabled" label.

Our evidence-based research tells us that the way out of the special education morass is to focus on better training of teachers and to shift the blame away from the one place it should never have been placed—the learners themselves. Teachers cannot impart information that they have never been taught. Continuing education can easily provide educators with the means to learn the latest findings and recommendations in the methodology and approach to teaching reading, and if we are to achieve the goal of teaching every child to read, then teachers' colleges should be held accountable in determining whether the methods they are currently imparting to future teachers will actually work in light of what science and research have categorically told us. Without a nationally mandated approach to teacher training, learners will continue to struggle, and educators will keep losing ground.

Few would argue that every individual needs to be literate in order to have equitable access to the civil rights and opportunities afforded them in this country. Some 50 years after the words "learning disabled" were first leveraged, we have reached an unprecedented place of national disparity. The gap between the haves and the have-nots has never been wider. The only universal equalizer that can mitigate this alarming gap is literacy. The ability to read is intertwined with every facet of our lives, from our right to vote and our potential for employment to our health and our personal safety. It is among the most basic of human rights, and yet for many Americans, it continues to be among the most elusive.

# INTERLUDE: "NATIVE ALIEN" BY JOHN CORCORAN

*Native alien here from there,*
*You can be found everywhere,*
*Going through the motions,*
*Showing your emotions.*

*Oh! Native alien, you are lame,*
*And literate society plays its games.*
*They still keep looking for someone to blame.*
*Isn't that the shame?*

*Don't they have any idea of our pain?*
*It seems so plain,*
*But they keep looking for someone to blame,*
*What a national shame.*

*They give us our promotions,*
*And put us through the motions.*
*Bluebirds here, redbirds there,*
*And now we have jailbirds everywhere.*

*Oh! How we tried!*
*Oh! How we cried!*
*We were just past five,*
*And how we had to hide!*

*Oh! How we had to hide!*
*Oh! How they stole our pride!*
*Oh! How they lied!*

*Native alien, here from there,*
*Native alien everywhere.*
*Shame, shame, we can't read,*
*And how this nation bleeds.*

*But they still will not heed,*
*Why Johnny the native alien,*
*Still can't read.*

*Oh! How we tried!*
*Oh! How many times has he died?*
*Literate society, you can't hide.*
*Oh! Literate society, how come you lie?*

*Scapegoat, cover up, alibi too.*
*Oh! Literate society, shame on you.*
*Oh! Literate society, you can't hide*
*Illiteracy statistics have your hide,*
*While you choke on your own pride.*

*Native alien, he can't read.*
*It limits him, we concede,*
*But he has ideas, concepts, and theories too!*
*And that's the stuff of thought,*
*That you ought to concede to.*

# CHAPTER FIVE

# Orality Morality

My move to St. Theresa's in the seventh grade had a profound, if short-lived, effect on my well-cultivated tough guy persona. The school had a crossing guard patrol, and for reasons I cannot remember, I applied to join. To my surprise and delight, I was accepted. The best thing about being a crossing guard was the uniform. The jacket was fire-engine red with shiny buttons, and the belt was pure white. The uniform practically broadcast the message that the person inside it was responsible, reliable, a helper. Tough guys weren't supposed to like feeling responsible, but I sure did. Our little platoon of about twelve received training from the local police department, and I took it very seriously—so seriously, in fact, that I earned the rank of Lieutenant, making me the officer in charge of the platoon. The rebels and the bullies might snicker at my smart red jacket, but I didn't care. I was doing things right. I was acting responsibly. I was demonstrating those oh-so-coveted leadership qualities. Me! Dumb Row Johnny!

Being a tough guy couldn't hold a candle to being a guy with leadership qualities. I loved my job and the feeling of accomplishment it gave me, because if I could do this, and do it right—make Lieutenant, for goodness' sake!—maybe I could do anything.

The sky was the limit until one day, when I reported for my crossing patrol shift and was told I had to turn in my uniform immediately. The nuns had reported to the patrol organizer that I wasn't working *hard enough in class and that my grades were poor—not the sort of person who should be on the crossing patrol. In silence, I handed over my belt and my red jacket, along with the only sense of self-worth I'd had in years.*

*I told myself I didn't care, that I'd expected this. Told myself the uniform hadn't quite fit right anyway, because like any loaner it wasn't made for me and it hadn't belonged to me—not the belt, or the coat, or the leadership qualities. I hadn't earned them; I was an impostor. Some other guy would come along who knew how to speak the language and surely knew how to read—one that fit the uniform perfectly.*

For untold centuries, most societies were based around spoken language and oral tradition. Language as we know it seems to be a uniquely human gift, and when we study it, we are uncovering something of the essence of human nature.

> **When written language overtook spoken language those who couldn't or didn't learn to read became disconnected from society.**

We know from our study of the brain that humans are not designed to be readers, but they do seem to be hardwired for language. Spoken language, like family and tribal ties, is a force that binds a culture together. Over time, written language overtook the oral tradition as the primary means of storing and transferring knowledge, and those who could not or did not learn to read then lacked a crucial connection to their own culture. In an oral tradition-based culture, those who could not hear might have experienced a sense of disconnection from their society. But does that mean the levels of disconnection of our hypothetical deaf citizen and a modern-day sub-literate citizen are equal? To answer that question, it is important to understand how and why man has communicated throughout the ages.

One of the oldest forms of human communication is speech. Language is a human creation, a tool that we invented to increase our safety, security, and prosperity. Language made society itself possible. We've established an understanding of how written language and the learned skill of reading changed our brains.

The converse is almost certainly true—in ancient oral tradition cultures, not only were human brains different, but the way in which humans thought was different. After centuries of literacy-centered tradition, most of us think in what could be described as prose. *This is a bad storm. I hope we don't lose power.* Those sentences could be someone's thoughts, or they could be lines of a novel, or a scribbled diary entry, or dialogue in a film. In cultures centered around spoken language (with no writing, and hence no reading), the process of thinking would have been very different—an outcome of speech rather than writing. It is impossible to say exactly how, but we do know why. If a culture's method of communicating affects every conceivable layer of a human's life experience, including the way they think, imagine how many obstacles both obvious and subtle must plague the illiterate and sub-literate in our society!

To get a sense of the consequences suffered by the illiterate and sub-literate person in a literacy-based culture, we need to first understand how our distant ancestors survived and flourished in pre-literate cultures. In any society, it is crucial to have a way to both store and transmit knowledge; storing of knowledge is vital to the survival of any group of people, as is a means of transmitting information to younger generations. The ancient Greeks, for example, developed what would seem to us to be an almost unbelievable discipline of memory. A huge amount of their historical and cultural knowledge was stored in epic works like *The Iliad*, which was memorized in full by bards, who would recite (or more accurately sing) the entire text to audiences—a process that could take over 25 hours from beginning to end. A recitation of this kind was a sophisticated performance, but the performance was not art in the sense that we know it; it was teaching, passing the information on in a way the audience could remember.

In the lifetime of Homer, author of the epic poems *The Iliad* and *The Odyssey*, the spoken poem was the most common delivery system of knowledge. An audience listening to a bard recite *The Iliad* was doing more than simply learning, however. They would experience the excitement, the fear, the triumph of the poem as it unfolded, becoming active witnesses to their own cultural roots. Every time an audience of Greek citizens gathered together in fellowship to witness these epics come to life, they strengthened their cultural bonds to one another in the process. They would return to their homes afterwards talking about what they'd heard, reciting parts of it to one another. Poetry was a glue that held their culture together.

Once a written alphabet was developed and introduced into a culture, the days of a spoken tradition were numbered. The arrival of written language is historically seen as tremendous leap forward, a development that paves the way for almost unlimited advances to come—and, of course, it is. But for some of the greatest thinkers of the time, written language was seen as something that would damage society as a whole and sabotage the human ability to think and learn. Socrates, for example, was a firm detractor of written language. A piece of writing, he said, could not explain itself to you. It was too limiting.

Furthermore, from Socrates' perspective, if people wrote everything down, they would destroy their own capacity for memory. This makes sense if you consider that if it is necessary to remember everything continually, a substantial amount of energy has to be expended to maintain the brain's capacity for memory. When such feats of memory are no longer necessary, energy is directed elsewhere and the capacity for memory shrinks. When we consider that the task of reciting *The Iliad* for 25 hours today would be considered virtually impossible, it's easier to understand why Socrates thought written language was a bad thing—it sabotaged a cognitive super-power. He was right, though he likely could not have imagined just how massively the literacy imprint would permeate the human experience.

In the 20th century, with the arrival of radio, the forgotten power of orality had a resurgence. Families in their own living rooms could listen to the sound of Hitler's voice delivering speeches halfway around the world, making speech a potent aural tool. More could be gleaned from that direct heard experience, the power and control Hitler held over the crowd, his ferocity, the crowd's fervent cheers, than any news article could communicate. One person could speak to all people for better, as in the case of Roosevelt's fireside chats and Martin Luther King's inspirational speeches, or for worse, like Hitler's demonic rhetoric.

**With the advent of technology as an integral part of our daily lives we no longer rely solely on our memory for information storage and retrieval.**

The advent of television, and ultimately computers and smartphones, served to further include the oral element, offering a platform for the written word, sound, and visual images (both photographs and video). Specified applications such as text-to-voice technology further broadened our means of transmitting information by allowing the visually-impaired to hear written text and to have their spoken words transcribed in writing—technology that has also been used extensively with sub-literate students. Technology has come full circle by reintroducing orality into our everyday lives.

As exciting as that is, though, it doesn't change the fact that our society is built on a foundation of literacy and is in many ways at its mercy. The 24/7 internet and smartphones have rewired our brains just as writing changed the brains of Socrates' fellow citizens. One of the simplest ways to demonstrate that is to consider how much less we now depend on our memories. Can we rattle off the phone numbers of our family and friends, or name each of their birth dates? Do we recall the driving route to a destination we visit once or twice every year? Almost every imaginable category of information can be summoned instantly on a phone or a laptop. Researchers have noted a corresponding drop in memory capacity, particularly of millennials, as well as a lessened ability to focus on one subject for a sustained period of time.

All of the wonderful inventions that continue to become available year after year—gadgets that can translate our words, convert our handwriting to type, dial a phone number with a voice command, recognize and identify a song on the radio in under five seconds—fail to change the isolation and shame so familiar to adults who are unable to read.

This brings us back to the question of whether a deaf person in an orally-based society experienced the same level of isolation and cultural disconnect as a non-literate person in today's literacy-based society. In light of this basic understanding of both, the answer must be a resounding "no." Our hypothetical deaf citizen of Homeric Greece could not hear a bard reciting one of the epics containing the essence of Greek knowledge and culture, but that would not have prevented him from attending such a recitation or from sitting in the audience with other citizens. He would be able to follow the words themselves by reading lips and feel and see the laughter, shock, or excitement of everyone around him. He would not be shut out of that crucial form of cultural bonding.

Orality is by nature a shared act. Literacy is by nature individual, undertaken alone. The modern-day person who can neither read nor write, therefore, is a cultural exile.

An illiterate or sub-literate person today has no choice but to attempt to function while embedded in a literate culture, but no matter what they do, they cannot truly share in the underlying social fabric that binds people together. As a result, a sub-literate person will always be at the mercy of society, isolated from the group in a severe and very dark way.

The primary means of communication in a society, whether spoken or written, provides a vital tool that admits an individual not just to the process of communicating, but provides membership to the whole club. The Greeks called their tool of speech *Logos,* and it was experienced as a godlike force—something that leapt out of one person's body, magically hurling through the air into the body of another person. The force of speech was considered a divine power. The sense of morality in the concept of orality is, for ancient cultures, absolutely obvious—self-evident. I believe that in the beginning was the word; God literally speaks the world into existence, and in the original Greek in which the Bible was written, that word is *logos*.

When writing supplanted speech, the necessary tool of citizenship and power changed from speaking/hearing to reading/writing—in other words, from a skill the brain was highly suited to master to a skill the brain was poorly suited to master. The associations the ancient Greeks made with orality, including the moral and civic importance of mastering the skill, were also transferred to reading and writing. In understanding the history of human communication and the reasons why the tool of communication is invested with pride and moral superiority, we begin to see the very ancient roots of shame in those who lack the tool.

As a result, the cards have long been stacked against the illiterate and sub-literate, and the consequences are broader and deeper than most people can imagine.

# INTERLUDE: "A TEACHER ON NAVIGATING THE LITERACY PARADOX" BY HOLLY MUELLER

During the first 16 years of my teaching career, I was looking for something. I didn't know what it was, but I knew there was something wrong with the way I was teaching my students to read and write. I remember four or five years ago when my first-grade teaching partner and I would chat for hours about this *thing* we were looking for. We didn't understand why we were telling our students "Go write!" when they couldn't decode simple words, or why we would tell students that the letter *a* makes a long and short sound, but when they read the word "*was*", it "just didn't follow the rules." I always felt that my students were learning to read in spite of what I was doing.

This all changed during my 17th year of teaching. That was the year my students no longer learned to read in spite of me; my students learned to read because of me. For the first time in my career, my students were reading BECAUSE OF ME!

A new principal had been hired that year. She was shocked when she saw the writing samples of our students. She didn't understand how we were sending kids off to read, yet we didn't teach them systematic strategies to decode. She mentioned bits and pieces about a system called EBLI: Evidence-Based Literacy Instruction. With each conversation we had, I knew this was what I had been looking for. The next summer I was trained in EBLI, and learned more in three days than I had in my entire master's program (which was a master's in reading!). I finally knew how to teach reading and writing. I finally knew how to be diagnostic with my readers.

EBLI has forever changed me. In parent/teacher conferences, parents would tell me their first-grader was reading better than their fourth-grader, and not a single parent told me their child complained about reading. On the contrary, parents reported children staying up past their bedtime to read! It may have taken

17 years, but I know there are many more children who will walk out of my classroom and will be reading *because of me*!

By the way, my teaching partner and I cannot believe the writing our kids are doing right now! They are writing all about books on topics they are researching. They are blowing us away!

# Silent Epidemic

*I*n my high school years, with the light at the end of the educational tunnel steadily growing brighter, my need to hide my truth and solidify my façade only grew more intense. I wanted desperately to be seen, to be recognized, but at the same time I could not bear to give up the phantom persona I had so exhaustively created and maintained. In my mind, the difference between those who had learned and those who had not was a bottomless canyon. My pretense had to be maintained no matter what, and there was only one way to do it. I cheated: cheated tests, cheated teachers, cheated my friends, cheated my family—cheated myself.*

*Each and every time I cheated, it created a feeling of anguish within me; this was not who or what I wanted to be. Trapped in the cycle, I did whatever was necessary to maintain the image of myself I had devised to hide my truth. Cheating to maintain that image became a language I mastered, intricately and effortlessly. The act of deception, large or small, was like a puzzle piece that seemed to fit the empty space in the center of the picture. Using deception in that way, I could fill the hole in the picture—I could cheat the image into completion. But in reality, the hole was still there.*

*This image of my impostor persona remained incomplete—its details not properly connected with that hole in the center, the gap that spoiled the whole delicate illusion. Deep in my gut, a similar hole was growing. It was a wound that ached and burned, a pain that kept me frozen in my weak imitation of the good boy. I did not try to make the pain go away, or expect the wound to heal. I didn't know that it could. It never got better, but it wasn't supposed to. It was mine, and I would carry it into adulthood as my own, understanding that something had given way at the center of my façade and now I was stuck with it.*

*There could be no going back.*

**12% of all American adults do not have basic literacy skills.**

The literacy initiatives and programs we are most likely to hear about and support are those geared towards our most vulnerable citizens—our children. While it is, of course, imperative to prioritize children in literacy programs, it can become far too easy to forget that an estimated 40 million American adults cannot read at or above a fifth-grade level, and that 50 percent of those adults cannot read at all. By that account, over 12 percent of all American adults have not been taught basic literacy skills.

It has become accepted in the terminology of literacy to refer to individuals reading at or below an elementary school level as "functionally illiterate." I want to say that I most emphatically dislike that term, because I believe very earnestly that words *do* matter. I identify strongly with the teachings of Socrates, particularly that "the beginning of wisdom is in the definition of terms."

To be wise in the issues of literacy, then, we must begin by carefully considering the words and labels we use. A "functioning alcoholic," for example, is a person who is impaired in some way by drinking, but who can get through their day in a normal fashion, go to work and drive to the supermarket, make dinner and take out the garbage. A person who might be considered "functionally illiterate" might also be able to get through their day in a normal fashion, but the similarity ends there. It's clear that when the word "functional" is paired with the word "alcoholic", the quality of the "functional" is a ruse; it creates a false appearance. A person who is "functional" is not optimum, not at their best; they are only just getting by. Their state and potential has been diminished. Life is, you assume, something of a struggle for

**Sub-literacy is a term describing anyone who is reading below their potential.**

them, and they are operating close to speed, but often just barely. Consider how you'd feel if you learned the pilot of a plane you were about to fly in was a functional alcoholic . . . For those reasons, I do not use the label of "functionally illiterate." I've always been more comfortable using plain "illiterate," but recently I have added the term "sub-literate", both because it has broader applications and is a more accurate descriptor.

Sub-literacy is a term describing anyone who is reading below their potential. The term covers a wide spectrum, from being able to read a small number of words to misreading or guessing many words, reading a comprehensive vocabulary slowly, having to reread passages often, not understanding or retaining what is read, and/or writing with consistent spelling inaccuracies. Those falling under the category of sub-literate might describe themselves in a variety of ways, such as "I don't like to read"; "I am a slow reader"; "I'm not a great reader"; or "I can never remember what I read." A habitually inaccurate speller might simply say, "I'm terrible at spelling," not understanding that the English language is a code with a logical decoding process, and that reading and spelling utilize the same code. Thus, inaccurate spellers are also not reading to their capacity. It is interesting to note that none of these descriptive statements individuals make of their sub-literacy imply any kind of disability or deficiency.

Often, clues of illiteracy and sub-literacy include some or all of the following: school age children might become easily distracted, misbehave, yawn, tell stories, become the class clown, need frequent bathroom trips, fidget, or develop headaches when they are asked to read. Adults might avoid writing lists, checks, notes, or anything requiring spelling. They often ask others to read things for them, use audiobooks exclusively, avoid reading by saying, "the print is too small", "I don't have my glasses", or some other avoidance tactic.

Children and adults have the ability to improve their reading by receiving instruction in how to understand the language decoding process used in reading and spelling. Some sub-literate adults do not even realize there is room for improvement, believing that they are just dumb or that reading—like athletics—is something some people naturally excel at and other people simply don't.

It was not until 1992 that the first serious study of illiteracy rates in American adults occurred, and another eleven years before the National Center for Education Statistics published a major undertaking of the national statistical picture with *Adult Literacy in America* in 2003. The study was the first to include specific details as to the skill levels of the adults who were interviewed, giving us a crucial view of how sub-literate and illiterate adults were represented by age, geographic location, income, and other factors. The study did not just provide percentages and trends; it examined literacy issues in the workforce, in cultural diversity, in the prison population, and in senior citizens.

As with the 1992 study, the 2003 statistics and numbers in *Adult Literacy in America* were quite daunting. Approximately 63 million adult Americans had only rudimentary literacy skills at an elementary school level—meaning they could do simple things such as fill out a deposit slip or read certain street signs, but could not read or write in any more complicated way. We've already explored a number of ways that children can and do slip through the educational cracks and become sub-literate or illiterate adults. But, when you're considering the full national scope of those who are sub-literate, it becomes apparent that there are other avenues to illiteracy and sub-literacy that are not surprising—students who drop out of school, for example, or students who were not native English speakers—and these only serve to widen the reach of sub-literacy so that ultimately there is no demographic that is immune.

It is happening in every socioeconomic group, in every state, in every school, and in every age group—I promise you that. Some might be surprised to learn that the data showed adults over the age of 65 were more likely to be sub-literate than middle-aged or younger adults. The more we look at studies like these and see for ourselves the broad spectrum of people who never learned to read, or to read well, the better prepared we are to take on the work of righting that wrong.

The study also created statistical pools to group and compare individuals by virtue of their native language and their race. Again, this is helpful primarily because it is not simply comparing have-nots to haves and perpetuating the myth that sub-literacy and illiteracy is a problem of the poor or the disadvantaged. The statistical pools demonstrate that even within a category organized around native languages, there are still patterns and tendencies that are the result of an endlessly complicated mesh of influence and inattention, of random chance and chronic cycles. In the statistical analysis of literacy levels in American Indian/ Alaskan Native, Hispanic, and Asian/Pacific Islander adults, factors determined to have contributed to the likelihood of failure to learn include the mother tongue and the educational norm in their birth country, as well as aspects of geography, economy, and politics that come into play at the local level.

Further, about 12 percent of the adults interviewed reported that they had "a physical, mental, or other health condition" that kept them from participating fully in work or other activities. These individuals were far more likely than adults in the population as a whole to rank in the two lowest performing literacy levels. There is one final group in the study I'd like to include in this chapter—a group that is better than any other in substantiating the kinds of factors that will affect an individual and render them less likely to learn: the group comprised of adults who are or have been incarcerated. As the researchers noted, "Adults in prison were far more likely than those in the population as a whole to perform in the lowest two literacy levels. These incarcerated adults tended to be younger, less well educated, and to be from minority backgrounds."

## Illiteracy and sub-literacy play a significant part in American adult male incarceration.

One thing almost all illiterate and sub-literate adults have in common is this: at some point they made their way into the adult world seeking to find a job and earn a living, to find a place to live, a community of friends, perhaps even a love interest, all while struggling (almost always silently) with insufficient literacy skills that created obstacle after obstacle in finding those things. Hindered at every turn, it is not uncommon for people to give up—to take a low-level job for which they are overqualified, or to stop looking for work at all. In some cases, with no means to get an income-generating job, they turn to crime. An adult male who is sub-literate or illiterate is statistically more likely to end up in jail than his literate twin brother.

The financial, medical, and emotional cost of adult illiteracy and sub-literacy is staggering. Labor statistics show the direct correlation between literacy levels and both salaries and rates of full-time employment falling as the literacy level falls. Adults who cannot read suffer a higher than statistically normal potential for developing behavior-related diseases such as diabetes and heart disease. They are more likely to suffer complications during medical treatment because of the inability to read medical directions and warnings. They are also more vulnerable to exclusion from insurance benefits, less able to capitalize on the rights guaranteed by insurance providers, and more likely to accept wrongly denied claims and bills generated in error. The illiterate or sub-literate adult is effectively barred from being a participating member of American society, and may be unable to use or enjoy the freedoms all Americans are guaranteed. They may not be able to vote, or to join an assistance program, or enroll their children in school.

To be illiterate as an adult—as I once was—is to be a person mired in silent shame, a keeper of secrets, a deviser of discreet short-cuts designed to hide our lack of literacy from friends, co-work-ers, or families. So, while it may come as a real surprise to learn that more than one in ten adult Americans are either illiterate or sub-literate, try to factor in how much time and effort they put into hiding their literacy difficulties. I can assure you that I did a masterful job of camouflaging it. We are right there among you, and we may look something like you; we may speak in the same way, but we who carry the secret of illiteracy *or* sub-literacy know that we are not like you or like everyone else. We know we are hopelessly different, and the shame of it is agonizing.

There is something else many people cannot fully grasp about people who learned to read later in life. For the many people like me, who began adulthood as sub-literate and then later learned to read and write, personal perspective gives stark evidence of how deeply our entire lives were shaped by the lack of literacy. Many people have shared my experience of finally learning to read; as a result, our outlook on life and the way we now see everything has changed drastically. Every person who has come to literacy in adulthood will have a vivid story of what it was like in that *before* time, of how oppressive this state of illiteracy or sub-literacy truly was—how it never let go, never got any better or easier to bear. And in that *after* time, reality seemed to change, and the world seemed to break open like a treasure chest—pride and self-esteem burst into blossom in our hearts.

In a way, learning to read as adults made us true citizens of the United States after decades of feeling like interlopers or squatters. It was only in hindsight that we could see the right to an edu-cation in literacy as a basic right, a civil right. To be sub-literate was to be plagued with an invisible affliction. Marginalized as we were, we had no way to truly process or understand the injustice that had been done to us when we were sent out into the world without the skills our education should have given us.

From this perspective, I understand why that shame was so pervasive, so much so that I still carry it three decades later. So insidious and toxic was that shame that I understand why so many people gave up, and why so many got angry or turned away from the law and moved to crime—and from crime, sadly, to prison.

How closely are illiteracy and crime related? Research indicates that they are deeply entwined with one another. Eighty-five percent of all juveniles who appear in the court system have literacy skills of elementary school level or lower. High school students with poor reading and writing skills are much more likely to give up on education and quit. High school dropouts are 63 percent more likely to spend time behind bars than their peers who go on to attend college. There is nothing subtle or open to interpretation in that data. The statistics go on for days, and they all bear out the truth of the correlation between illiteracy and crime, and between illiteracy and educational dropouts.

In his book *Essentials of Assessing, Preventing, and Overcoming Reading Difficulties*, David Kilpatrick notes that "It is difficult to overestimate the importance of reading for success in school and in life. Reading is essential for all academic subjects. Science and social studies require textbook reading. Many math tests, including state-level assessments, require students to read word problems. Poor reading virtually guarantees poor writing skills. As a result, reading affects a student's entire academic experience."

In developed countries, the level of an individual's literacy skill is proportionate to their income level (and inversely proportional to the risk of committing crime), taking the already uneven playing field of sub-literacy and filling it with so many barriers and obstacles there is virtually no escape. This is as well-known in the law enforcement community as it is in the educational world. The Department of Justice has been quoted as saying "The link between academic failure and delinquency, violence, and crime is *welded to reading failure.*"

Welded. That's a powerful term. The message cannot be stated much more categorically than that.

You may wonder why organizations like the NCES or non-profit organizations like Room to Read, the San Diego Council on Literacy, or my own John Corcoran Foundation, keep revisiting the territory of adult illiteracy *and* sub-literacy. The reason is simple. It is imperative that people be made to understand the human truth behind all these statistics—namely, how powerful the force and duration of financial, medical, and psychological sabotage are, and what that does to every person who leaves school without literacy skills—and how the effect is so profound it does not stop with the individual, but ripples outward like shockwaves over the nation as a whole. The fallout of adult illiteracy is *that* bad; it is *that* powerful. It is a game-changer at every level of our society, and that message must be heard not just by educators, policymakers, and volunteers—it must reach the sub-literate adults themselves. For so many, the cloak of shame worn for so many years will not be removed, and help is never sought. Shame begets silence, and silence begets the status quo.

David Kilpatrick writes, "It has been shown in multiple empirical studies that a large proportion of students at risk for reading difficulties, as well as students with severe reading disabilities, can develop and maintain normal reading skills when provided with the right kind of intervention." Knowing this, why would such intervention not become a top priority both with schools and with policymakers?

I understand people are faced with countless problems and issues and crises (whether their own, the country's, or the world's), and it is impossible to take action to mitigate more than a handful. I understand that my urgency to spread this message and get these adults to programs that will help is unique to me, because I was once one of them. My language is one of experience, so by its nature it is not universal or even widely relatable. But almost everyone, young or old, struggling or coasting, can speak and relate to the language of money; and in those monetary terms, the message is just as clear. Spending associated with the problems of illiteracy and sub-literacy cost American taxpayers billions of dollars each year. For example, social service spending and decreased tax revenue that are the result of students who drop out of school come with a whopping $240 billion price tag every year.

A 2013 Rand Corporation study demonstrated that by taking part in either academic or vocational

**The subliterate among us are often less affluent, prone to illness, run afoul of the law, and need more assistance as they grow older than their literate counterpart.**

education programs offered in prison, there was a corresponding 40% drop in recidivism. In monetary terms, that translated into future savings of an estimated four to five dollars for every dollar spent on prison education. They say money talks, and it's certainly doing it here—loud and clear. Literacy creates money, and illiteracy and sub-lilteracy consume it.

Reading and writing—and, more specifically, being provided an education in which all people can learn those skills—are inalienable human rights. Every person who reaches adulthood without literacy skills is a person carrying an invisible and backbreaking burden. The illiterate and sub-literate will be poorer than us, sicker than us, weaker than us—and they will need more help than we do now, they will be more likely to run afoul of the law, and they will need more help than we will when they grow old. And yet, their burdens can be easily lifted. They can *still* learn to read and write; it isn't too late, and programs that will work for them are within everyone's reach. The illiterate and sub-literate can become literate, no matter what, and it is their right to do so, but it is also our responsibility to help make that happen. If we do not, the social, spiritual, and financial cost will be so high we will set our nation on a collision course with bankruptcy of spirit, bankruptcy of flesh, and bankruptcy of prosperity. And that is a burden none of us can afford to bear.

# Interlude: "A Parent on Family Literacy" by Tina

I still get choked up when I think back to the day, just before Halloween of his first-grade year, when Spencer said, "Mom, I am the lowest reader in my class." After investigating, I realized his statement was accurate—and the beginning of a long, painful journey. As a former teacher, I felt punched in the gut. Somehow, I didn't notice Spencer's struggles as I busily raised three young boys. I hadn't noticed that he was memorizing words, and his memory was maxed out.

Spencer and I went round and round his first-grade year as I tried helping him learn to read. He would cry and get frustrated working through unknown words. No matter what I tried, I couldn't reach him.

Fall conferences in second grade had me holding back tears. The student described was not our son. Spencer, though very intelligent, was not engaging in class discussions, was acting out, and was struggling. There was a suspected attention issue due to classroom behaviors.

Throughout second grade, homework time was so stressful. Spencer would act out to avoid admitting he didn't know something. He felt inferior to his peers, and was bothered by classmates who experienced success. Spencer's teacher stood by us, doing all she could to help; however, it wasn't until he received intense reading intervention at a local private reading center that his life completely changed. He finally learned to read! Spencer's confidence increased, he participated in class discussions, his grades began to soar, and homework times improved. He even chose reading for entertainment!

Spencer is nearing the end of his third-grade year. My tears flowed again after spring conferences, but this time it was after hearing his teachers say that Spencer is at grade level now, works well with his classmates, and his contributions to discussions are an asset to the class. I am so proud of his perseverance at such a young age!

CHAPTER SEVEN

# Operative Advantage

*J*ust before my senior year in high school was to begin, my family relocated again, to Parker, Arizona. Arizona agreed with me from day one. I got myself a job hauling hay and managed to catch the attention of a blue-eyed girl named Mildred. After a considerable investment of my wages in movie tickets and drugstore sodas, Mildred and I were going steady. It was as if we were made for one another. I was a big achiever on the football field and basketball court, while Mildred was head majorette. She was popular and beautiful. Also, I made friends fast, had been given to understand I was not exactly hard on the eyes, and was even voted homecoming king. But Mildred was an academic achiever, not just because she was organized and could type a mile a minute—Mildred was SMART. How was I going to keep my secret if I had a smart, book-reading girlfriend? I was worried enough that I started praying pretty hard on the subject every day. But even in my prayers, I couldn't quite imagine how I could learn to read unless it happened by way of a genuine miracle, New Testament style. So I suppose what I was praying for was to wake up one morning and pick up a book, and everything would instantly fall into place and I would begin to read. Maybe it was Arizona; there was something about this place, this school, this year, this girl—it was all so right, *so perfect. If a miracle were going to happen, why not here, where life seemed authentic and decent and filled with promise? Why not now?*

*And maybe it would have. Maybe that miracle was on its way. But halfway through the school year, my father got a new job, starting immediately, in California. We were moving again, and I would lose Mildred and my teammates and my friends, and with them the last possibility that my affliction might be healed by divine intervention.*

All great undertakings begin with a simple seed, whether it is a shared experience, a tragedy, a miraculous occurrence, or the simple purity of altruism and the desire to be of some help in the world. As a young man, I had no particular desire to volunteer for anything. I was more than willing to work, but I wanted to be paid for my efforts. It was not until my own life was transformed by volunteers that both my path and my destination began to become clear to me.

I was 48 years old when I met literacy volunteer Eleanor Condit at the Carlsbad Library Learning Center. Eleanor loved to read, and she didn't think anyone should go through life without that ability. That simple but deep-rooted belief that literacy was a fundamental component of equality was the seed of Eleanor's passion, and the reason that she volunteered. While Eleanor's name may not appear in the history books as someone who changed the world, she most certainly changed mine in the most profound way, helping me to unlock the mysteries of the printed word.

Though I did not know it at the time, this was the beginning of my own evolution as a volunteer. While entrenched as I was in the trauma of decades of illiteracy/sub-literacy, Eleanor acted as a kind of first responder, giving me the immediate aid I needed to become stabilized. Literacy volunteers are a great boon, but they are not the answer to America's literacy crisis. The literacy corps is a reminder that we are in crisis and something needs to be done about it. These volunteers have taken the leadership initiative to make the call, focusing the national spotlight as they showcase some of their stories.

There is a widespread misconception that volunteers can do all of the work. This is often not the case, and it is an unfair burden to place on volunteers but, among other things, it creates a sense of complacency that the problem is under control. Eleanor Condit worked for thirteen months with me, getting my skills to about a sixth-grade level.

**If you want to help solve the problems of the world, begin by working to solve them in your own community.**

She then had the extraordinary wisdom to understand I needed to be directed to the next step, and the next guide. That person turned out to be Pat Lindemood, who had developed a three-tiered approach to sensory-cognitive instruction—first teaching the ability to perceive sounds within words, then creating a mental image of the spellings of those sounds (making the connection of the spelling to a word), and finally creating a mental concept of the meaning of the whole word. And *it worked*.

Now I knew through my own direct experience that there was a solution to our literary crisis. There was a method of instruction capable of succeeding with a student for whom all traditional means had failed. I was the living proof. This discovery was as significant for me as it might be to find a recipe for a potion that cured cancer. It ignited the embers of a passion I had not previously experienced—to connect the students with the solution.

Not only did I want to continue learning, I wanted to join the ranks of volunteers. I wanted to be one of the people who helped. I began in the same way all grassroots movements do: in my own back yard, with the San Diego Council on Literacy.

Microbiologist and environmentalist René Dubos—who won a Pulitzer Prize in 1969—popularized the environmental precept "Think globally, act locally." The logic is simple: If you want to help solve the problems of the world, begin by working to solve them in your own community. It is the adage that fuels all grassroots movements. The term "grassroots" is thought to have been first used in a political sense in 1912 by Indiana senator Albert Beveridge, who said of his Progressive Party, "This party has come from the grass roots. It has grown from the soil of people's hard necessities." The words could just as easily be applied to literacy; for millions unable to read above a rudimentary level, the need to learn is a hard necessity indeed.

But if, as I had discovered, instructional methods already existed to teach those whom traditional instruction had failed, why were they not being used as traditional instruction for everyone? More troubling, why were these methods not being made available to those who most urgently needed them? As my own volunteering efforts evolved from speaking engagements to the establishment of the John Corcoran Foundation, I continued to struggle with that question. At the time, I didn't know where the John Corcoran Foundation would lead—it was simply my response to what was happening. I had heard the call, and I was answering it because I wanted to serve as a model the way Eleanor Condit had for me. When the Foundation was up and running, we did not yet have the full scope of our mission statement developed. We had fairly universal agreement that education and reading were prerequisites, and widespread acknowledgment that reform was needed. We also knew we had a sound scientific basis from which to approach the crisis.

We searched and researched and hypothesized until our objective evolved to include three elements: awareness of the problem, solutions to the problem, and instruction to implement the solution. The result of that evolution was a mission statement that was boldly clear: to provide effective, one-on-one literacy instruction to any person who wanted to learn to read. The key to accomplishing our mission was finding and adopting an effective instructional method, and ensuring that our staff was properly trained to employ that method. Now we were ready to get to work.

The Foundation put me on the front lines armed with grant funding, a proven instruction method, and qualified individuals ready to teach. It was there on the front line that I discovered for myself exactly why it was so difficult to get the instructional solution to the student. The entire process, steeped in bureaucracy and riddled with red tape, seemed to have been designed to thwart us. Why? It seemed evident that in some districts, they really wouldn't or couldn't acknowledge the crisis and accept that they were not effectively teaching students to read.

There is a sense of conspiracy that seems to be a dominant factor in preventing educators from admitting the scope of the literacy crisis. Having spent so much of my life centering on shame-based actions to hide my own illiteracy/sub-literacy, I understood the destructive power of pride. To hide the problem, one must create a reality in which there is no problem. This would prove to be daunting to us at the John Corcoran Foundation when we were ready to bring our program to students.

Every state has a different process for deeming an organization "qualified" and giving them state certification, and the same process must be repeated for individual districts—and that is only the beginning of the hurdles. In one district, for example, we needed to provide an arduous 100 pages of documentation to get approval. All of that work only made us eligible to compete with others for contracts, which schools would bid on using federal money allocated for that specific purpose—and it wasn't optional. When federal funds are given for a specific purpose, they have to be used. What we discovered was that school administrations weren't exactly happy about the extra work this required of them.

Parents in the district are the ones who actually choose what program best matches their children. When our program was chosen, we were ready to get to work, only to discover that this particular district had a policy that volunteer organizations could not use school classrooms. In fact, they would not allow us on campus *at all*. We were forced to find rental space and contend with the nightmare of coordinating transportation for the students. To smooth the way and facilitate incentive for families, we began to offer every student who signed up with us a computer, which would be delivered and connected to the internet at our own expense; and if the student completed the program, the computer would be theirs to keep. To our astonishment, it began to get back to us that some district faculty members were telling parents that our promise was bogus, and that we had no intention of honoring it.

It was clear to us that it was going to be very difficult to partner with schools who did not want the bother of having us there. It was tremendously demoralizing—worse than being kept out of the schools. The system was in place to allow us to do exactly what we were trained to do, but having led the educational horse to water, we found it was virtually impossible to induce it to drink. When and how had the educational system become so rigid, so utterly dedicated to promoting illiteracy?

The "when" is debatable, but it was clear that the "how" was a corps of teachers who hadn't been taught what they need to effectively teach all of their students to read. They were also under supported, understaffed, and overwhelmed by state regulations and testing—and further hobbled by individuals and organizations that stood to profit from the status quo. As discouraged as I was, I could understand the fatigue and disillusionment that was giving rise to such a stubborn level of stasis. It seemed inevitable, then, that more of the burden to initiate change would have to fall on individuals and organizations outside of the public education system. It was painfully clear that a significant reform effort was required. Yet with an illiteracy and sub-literacy crisis that was evidently going to continue growing, literacy seemed to be the elephant in the room that no one discussed when people talked of reform.

**A key indicator of whether or not a child will graduate from high school is the ability to read at a fourth grade reading level.**

Journalist Juan Williams wrote an op-ed piece for the *Wall Street Journal* in July of 2016 in which he stated that the ending of another school year marked another lost opportunity for millions of students, most especially minority students who bore the brunt of the suffering. The article cites a report showing that only 21% of Hispanic fourth-grade students were considered "proficient" in reading. "This is bad news," Williams wrote. "A fourth-grader's reading level is a key indicator of whether he or she will graduate from high school." African-American fourth-graders performed even worse—a mere 18% of them were deemed proficient. And it's clear as it's ever been that the issue does not discriminate. Williams notes, "Only 46% of white fourth-graders—and 35% of fourth-graders of all races—were judged 'proficient' in reading in 2015."

The report Williams referenced showed that far too many American children were failing to achieve their potential, and that the impact on African-American students was the most severe; and yet African-American students have no special predilection for difficulty in learning—the impact of educational failure on minorities is almost entirely a function of politics, poverty, and location. The schools in the poorest areas with the poorest families are often the schools that are the least able to afford to research and implement targeted solutions. In fact, the fallout of the faltering education system is felt most intensely by minorities, though the numbers differ greatly from state to state. The white population is also feeling the fallout, but both schools and parents themselves have learned to camouflage it better.

I was a white male with a college-educated father, and I didn't learn to read in all my years from kindergarten through high school, nor did I learn in college. The fact that I was able to learn to read at the age of 48 makes it obvious that I was a capable enough student. Illiteracy and sub-literacy do not discriminate. Regardless of race, creed, socioeconomic status, or gender, there are people in your life (and likely even your family) who have difficulty with reading and writing. Sub-literate people who are prominent businessmen, engineers, medical students, lawyers, inventors, judges, and psychologists have all sought out the instruction provided by the John Corcoran Foundation over the years because they were not reading proficiently and wanted help. They didn't want anyone to know about it. They felt ashamed and embarrassed.

The statistics are grim, and all the more agonizing given the fact that the solution is there for the taking. Millions continue to be

**Throwing money at the literacy/sub-literacy crisis is not the answer.**

locked out of organizations that exist to help them. Inequities in the justice system, and unemployment and dropout rates, are not in and of themselves the problem; they are the result of rampant illiteracy and sub-literacy. As Williams article shows, ground zero of the epidemic is our local elementary schools. What would it take to break this cycle?

I knew the answer before I was consciously aware of it. The educational system is the proverbial battleship that will take a long time to change direction even after the course has been altered. Until our universities begin to train teachers in the latest evidence-based research to teach all learners at every ability level, we have to look outside the educational system for transitional help.

We all need to step into our own backyards and tap into the resource growing right out of the soil—our grass roots. The onus is now on the non-educator community to step up in any number of ways, from individuals identifying and supporting local literacy organizations, volunteers researching effective programs and pitching in, and churches and other community groups offering classes to the technology industry developing and supporting literacy programs and helping to get computers into disadvantaged students' homes. Acting locally is our only viable resource, and for most people it will not cost a dime.

Contrary to popular belief, throwing money at the literacy crisis doesn't seem to help. We spend more money per capita on education than any other country in the world. Clearly money is not the problem here. While we cannot stop looking to the government to facilitate the change to the system, we do not have the luxury of waiting for that to happen. We have to start ourselves, in our backyards, fueled by necessity and faith that our efforts will take root. As it says in the Talmud, "Every blade of grass has its angel that bends over it and whispers, 'Grow. Grow.'"

The literacy movement already has its fair share of angels helping it to grow. I'm privileged to know many of them personally. Maria Murray, a professor of literacy at SUNY Oswego, founded an organization called The Reading League, an organization devoted to advancing evidence-based reading practices in schools through social media, networking, and professional development. The Reading League is comprised of teachers, professors, researchers, administrators, parents, people with reading difficulties, and more.

Another literacy angel is Patricia Smart, the founder and developer of Author Adventures, which provides a virtual visit to the homes and landmarks of some of America's best-loved writers. This project inspires readers and brings some of the best-loved places in fiction to life, such as Orchard House, the real-life home of Louisa May Alcott's *Little Women,* and the historic homes of *Little House on the Prairie* author Laura Ingalls Wilder.

Jose L. Cruz is one of our senior angels, currently Chief Executive Officer of the San Diego Council on Literacy. He has devoted more than 30 years of his life to the field of education and has organized collaborative literacy programs on a national level. He's served as president of the San Diego branch of the International Dyslexia Association and the National Alliance of Urban Literacy Coalition, and is a past winner of the *San Diego Union-Tribune*'s "Educator of the Year" award and the International Reading Association's "Celebrate Literacy" award.

There are many, many more. With so many passionately committed individuals acting as trailblazers by answering the call, there is reason for optimism. As Nora Chahbazi, founder of the EBLI: Evidence-Based Literacy Instruction program and the Ounce of Prevention Reading Center, wrote after attending a Reading League event: "Hearing about this newly formed literacy organization, their altruistic goals, and their very well-attended events gave me hope: hope because there are others devoting their time and energy to the mission of literacy for all, asking for nothing in return; hope that teachers would have greater access to literacy instructional practices that work; hope that students would be taught to accurately and successfully read, write and spell; hope that those looking at the issue of illiteracy or sub-literacy will be met with the question 'What do WE (me included) need to do differently?' as opposed to labeling, decreasing expectations, and/ or blaming students for their deficiencies; hope because there was a large and great group of people looking to promote and provide solutions that work."

So even as the door of educational institutions closes to outside literacy efforts, hope has opened a window, and visible through that window is a great human chain of individuals like Maria, Patricia, Jose, and Nora, partners and pioneers of new solutions. At the John Corcoran Foundation we continued to evolve, searching for and finding a form of literacy instruction and training that we knew was effective: Nora Chahbazi's EBLI program. This new circle of support became complete with the realization of a factor so massively galvanizing it rendered the grassroots literacy movement virtually unstoppable. The galvanizing force is technology.

A young social activist named Vivienne Harr, who famously opened a "Make a Stand" lemonade stand which raised $100,000 to free children in slavery, wrote, "Technology connects us. Technology unites us. Technology amplifies our power." I don't think anyone could have said it better. It was technology, we realized at the Foundation, that was our way back in. The Reading League, Author Adventures, and EBLI all centered on or offered online content, available to anyone on the internet.

In EBLI we had found an evidence-based system of reading instruction that we knew worked, not just for kids but for teachers. It wasn't the first, and certainly there are others—as I knew personally, since Pat Lindamood's sensory-cognitive method had worked for me. But the age-old problem had been how to connect the effective system with the student who needed it. Besides in-person teacher training and student instruction, EBLI has developed a series of apps that readers of any age can download and use.

This coming together of people and the amplifying power of technology enabled the John Corcoran Foundation to make its most significant evolutionary advance to date.

We became true believers in online content.

## INTERLUDE: "A NOTE FROM THE PRINCIPAL" BY MARK THOMAS

The noted author and Ted Talk presenter, Dr. Brene Brown, says that "vulnerability is our most accurate measure of courage." I agree with her wholeheartedly. Based on my belief in her statement, John Corcoran is without question one of the most courageous people I have ever had the pleasure to meet. John demonstrates that courage repeatedly laying himself bare when it comes to being vulnerable about his lifelong relationship with reading and the turmoil that dysfunctional relationship created in his life.

I had the pleasure to meet John a few years back when he spoke to my teaching staff at Northview High School. He was on a visit to Michigan early in his collaboration with Nora Chahbazi and her Evidence Based Literacy Instruction (EBLI) program. John had the rapt attention of his audience as he spoke. His authenticity and vulnerability were palpable. I could feel that some of the teachers were uncomfortable and empathetic to his struggles. Looking back, I can now see that John knew his path to helping others and self-healing required him to "come out of the shadows" about the issue of illiteracy by telling his story. After reading *The Teacher Who Couldn't Read*, listening to John speak, and having a conversation with him, it was apparent that John had been using his personal journey to create awareness and action on the issue. He was also making it safe for others who could hopefully realize that they are not alone nor are they to blame.

What I have now realized about John was that he has been working on two issues and important causes simultaneously . . . one is the subject of illiteracy and its solution, and the other is his psychological/emotional health during his lifelong personal journey with reading and everything that connects to it.

In many ways I see John's story as one of a cancer survivor who has beaten the odds, lived to tell the tale and now wants to put out a clarion call to address the issue. The literacy/illiteracy story in our society has many things in common with what our medical professionals deal with regarding disease with one very important exception . . . we have found a cure for illiteracy and "sub-literacy" (as John so accurately refers to reading below expected level) but the powers that be in our nation have yet to demonstrate the "political will" to mandate and share the cure.

The concept of having people, both individually and collectively, admit to failing so many kids and families for so many years when it comes to ineffective programs, tools and practices related to reading is completely foreign to us in our society. It is rare to find a leader or an organization given responsibility for the well-being of others who, without some public provocation or impetus by emergency, stands up to take accountability for their failures. It is just as rare to find that leader or organization who is also committed to taking positive actions moving forward to help improve or resolve the issue. The reason for this paralysis you ask . . . because it would take an uncommon display of vulnerability.

John Corcoran is unique in that he was not a perpetrator but a victim. He also realized that most of the perceived perpetrators were "unwitting accomplices" in that they were conditioned to teach in a manner that promoted struggle for some because they just didn't know any better. He also knew there were others who likely were aware of the ineffectiveness, but various factors usually related to money, power, influence and potential embarrassment kept them quiet. It was that last factor, potential embarrassment, that John was willing to take on by going public with his story.

John was not on a mission of revenge or spite in regard to those that had failed him in his goal to be a reader over the course of his lifetime. To be fair though, he was also not conducting a "blameless autopsy" of his journey or those of others related to illiteracy and sub-literacy. Instead, he chose to focus on offering grace by sharing his story which includes such things as victim blaming and self-loathing as a means to cope with the trauma.

The sad irony we see in that process is that it is the victims often assign themselves blame and responsibility for the crime because rarely has anyone accepted responsibility, offered an apology and sought positive resolution. Even though research favorably supports this practice, it requires the offending party to become vulnerable by admitting their wrong, enduring the guilt and shame, apologizing to the victim and collectively creating a solution in order to restore goodwill moving forward. Unattainable . . . no way. Undesirable, often, because as Brene Brown points out it requires vulnerability, guilt and shame prior to achieving courage.

I would describe John as an individual who has not only found his voice but, much more importantly, found his inner peace through his journey of vulnerability giving him the freedom to step up on his bully pulpit and demonstrate the type of courage it will take to give everyone in our nation and world the gift of reading.

My sincere hope is that John's powerful example will be replicated by others moving forward. I do believe there are many people who care about improving illiteracy and sub-literacy, but I also think it is an "accepted failure of society" just like hunger, racism and healthcare issues in our country because resolving it would require massive amounts of vulnerability and that thought makes many people highly uncomfortable.

What I will "settle for" though is that John and other "teaching the world to read" advocates like him can generate a "re-awakening" on the topic of literacy centered on a re-examination of what we now know related to reading instruction in addition to what we now understand regarding the unique challenges faced by many parts of our population. If we could hit reset and revise our resource allocation based on supporting successful research-based practices/tools combined with improved teacher training using these methods I share John's hope that great progress can be achieved.

# CHAPTER EIGHT

# Act Locally

*T*hough California had never been the subject of my dreamin',
I found the town of Blythe pleasant enough. The high school
was refreshingly diverse, unlike any of the schools I'd previously attended, and I made friends easily in the few months before
graduation. I was filled with anticipation at the prospect of getting
my high school diploma. It had been such a struggle to keep up the
façade, but now, with diploma in hand, I had the chance to make
something of myself—to fulfill the promise of my abilities, and in
doing so perhaps make up for some of the wrong I had done. I was
so excited about graduation that I invited Mildred to attend. The
moment I crossed the stage with diploma in hand, I was soaring
with happiness. As the ceremony ended, I unrolled the diploma so
that I could have a look at it. My happiness vanished and I came
crashing down to earth. The diploma in my hands was blank. I had
some incomplete credits, and no one had bothered to tell me.

I attended summer school, then graduated from high school in
1956. At that time, America was experiencing the beginning of
a technological revolution so massive, almost every aspect of
human life would in some way be changed by it. The advent of
computers and related technology had as profound an impact on
our society as did the Industrial Revolution of the 19th century. As
a teenager, I could not have even parsed the concept of the internet. We had the marvelous invention of the talking box, followed

by the talking box with moving pictures; what could there possibly be left to invent?

In a newspaper article for a 1936 issue of *The Delineator*, reporter Jessie Wiley Voiles had this reaction to watching television demonstrated for the first time: "In the semi-darkness we sat in tense silence waiting to see the premiere demonstration of television...Television! What would it be like? I remembered how miraculous the first radios seemed...Suddenly, there in the lid of the wonder machine appeared the small but clear image of Betty Goodwin, television announcer, sent out on the air from the Empire State Building dome." By 1958, 82% of American homes had at least one television, a dramatic increase from one decade earlier, when less than 1% of households owned what in the early days was called a "home screen."

When *Sesame Street* arrived on the scene in 1969, we had our first real look at how the technology of television could provide a valuable and high-quality educational experience for young children. As described by the National Center for Learning Disabilities' website Get Ready to Read, "Each 60-minute show is backed by a curriculum, which is grounded in years of research and continuous work with educational experts. Through this work with teachers, researchers, and parents, *Sesame Street* continues to evolve . . . Each episode is stocked with reasoning games, sounding out letters and words, counting, pattern recognition and other important early literacy and math skills appropriate for children ages 4-7 years old." A 2013 analysis published in the *Journal of Applied Developmental Psychology* confirms that after four decades, "*Sesame Street* is an enduring example of a scalable and effective early childhood educational intervention. The significant, positive effects on cognitive learning

> **Children who watched educational television at the age of 2–3 are better prepared for school and perform better on tests.**

and socio-emotional outcomes observed . . . represent real educational benefits for the millions of preschool-age children around the world who visit *Sesame Street* via their televisions." Another profoundly successful educational program, *Reading Rainbow*, focused solely on reading, and a 1977 Corporation for Public Broadcasting study found that teachers who used educational programming in the classroom rated it the best.

In 2001, a study was published in *Child Development* that demonstrated that children who watched educational television at ages 2-3 were better prepared to transition into school and performed better on tests. The report further suggested that "When children enter school, those with good school-readiness skills are likely to have more experiences of success and to be perceived by teachers as more able, perhaps starting a trajectory of better performance and higher levels of academic motivation than children who enter with poor skills."

That is a rather significant finding—documented evidence that children's entire educational path can be positively affected during this "early window." A technological device already found in over 95% of all U.S. households could, when paired with quality educational programming, improve the learning skill set of young children and help them prepare for the transition into school. A factor that works in television's favor is that it is a self-initiating activity that requires nothing else by way of materials or adult supervision. But one crucial factor works against it—a factor that has been demonstrated to positively impact learning ability and language skills: in television there is no interactivity with the viewer. The watching experience remains the same, and cannot be affected by the progress or the interest of the watcher.

To me, the VCR was a miraculous device that assisted me in teaching my high school students. The miniseries *Roots* was instrumental in creating a rich, open dialogue between my students and me in a race relations course I taught in the mid-1970s. I would record the show at home and show it to my students the following day. This melded beautifully with my style of teaching, which included lots of discussion and visual aids and avoided print.

Following the introduction of the personal computer in 1975, the devices have enjoyed a meteoric rise in popularity to this day. My first experience with computers was for accounting in my business. I began using them for reading and writing in the late '90s, after I'd had time to hone my newly acquired literacy skills.

By this time, it was very common to own a computer, but statistics show that even today they are not quite as prevalent as televisions in U.S. households. While only 5% of homes have no television, the U.S. Census shows that 25% of households do not have a computer. Statistics also show that of school age children between the ages of 3-17, 83.2% have access to a computer at home, and increasing numbers also have access at school. It's quite clear this is not a passing trend; computers and digital technology are here to stay. How do we best leverage the fact that someone who is not proficient in literacy (reading and writing below grade level) can very likely operate a computer or a smartphone? The question points to the gulf between what educational consultant Marc Prensky calls digital natives (children inhabiting the digital landscape from birth) and digital immigrants (those born before the 21st century and who were not brought up with technology). Many teachers who are digital immigrants struggle to learn and apply new information and communications technology. These digital natives are engaging with technology at earlier and earlier ages. Whether they have any previous reading or writing skills, many come to school comfortable with the digital language of computers, video games, and the internet.

It's now understood that substantial use of computer and digital technology does result in changes to the human brain, much in the way the activity of reading changes our cognitive hardwiring. This fact is especially significant for children whose brains are both undergoing development and

**eBooks increase student motivation to read.**

are in a period of heightened neuroplasticity. It's a double-edged sword. In a 2012 article in *Psychology Today,* Jim Taylor writes, "There is, however, a growing body of research that technology can be both beneficial and harmful to different ways in which children think. Moreover, this influence isn't just affecting children on the surface of their thinking. Rather, because their brains are still developing and malleable, frequent exposure by so-called digital natives to technology is actually wiring the brain in ways very different than in previous generations." Clearly it is more important than ever to pursue educational computer programs that have their basis in sound scientific fact and proven success.

How can we hope to keep struggling readers interested in the face of so much competition from television and video games? Fortunately, the genre of children's books has fostered some ingenious creativity in electronic (or eBook) adaptations. Some eBooks use animation and other digital techniques to create interactive components in the artwork, and to provide an additional layer to the story. A 2012 literacy survey by the National Literacy Trust found that the use of eBooks increased student motivation to read, especially in those considered struggling readers.

Maryanne Wolf, director of the Center for Reading and Language Research at Tufts University, states, "We have to move into the 21st century, but we should do so with great care to build a 'bi-literate' brain that has the circuitry for 'deep reading' skills, and at the same time is adept with technology." She goes on to add, "It seems probable that more effective schools and teachers are more likely to use digital technologies more effectively than other schools. We need to know more about where and how it is used to greatest effect, then investigate to see if this information can be used to help improve learning in other contexts."

In the John Corcoran Foundation's evolution, we had previously noted the prevalence of gatekeepers in our educational system, and we had devised the tutoring program to get around them— only to be thwarted by red tape and unenthusiastic school systems. It was tremendously frustrating, especially as I knew from experience that there were effective solutions out there—teaching methods that were successful with people like me, for whom previous instruction had failed. Increasingly aware that the internet was a gatekeeper-free medium, the Foundation began to focus on developing technology specifically designed to bring the student and the solution together in cyberspace.

While we were piecing together instruction that consisted of commercial software programs combined with real-time Skype instruction and support for students, we continued to search to improve the instruction we were providing. In a tremendous moment of serendipity, it was at this juncture that my path crossed with that of Nora Chahbazi and her Evidenced-Based Literacy Instruction (EBLI), a system of strategies that was producing startling results. The following description of EBLI by Nora describes how the program does it.

*Currently, literacy instruction in schools focuses mostly on comprehension without sufficient instruction on how to manage the alphabetic code to accurately read the words before moving on to accessing meaning from text. Students are encouraged to guess words as they read and invent spelling as they write. Typically, incorrect reading and incorrect spelling of words are reinforced.*

*To learn to read and write, students need a system that helps them make sense of the code. Immediate error correction is imperative. EBLI provides teachers with the research-based theory, skills, concepts, and practice to effectively and efficiently teach students how to read, write, and spell correctly from the onset. The multimodal and highly engaging lessons ensure that all students are interactively learning in ways that meet their needs. The EBLI system is easily integrated into daily instruction across all grade levels, in any subject that requires reading, writing, or spelling.*

*Students quickly learn the English alphabetic code so accurate reading is imprinted. Spelling patterns are taught in the context of writing and misspelled words are corrected immediately. Correct writing conventions are modeled and practiced and again, mistakes are corrected as they happen. Applying what has been learned by reading in text and writing for a purpose is a crucial component of EBLI. The results: All students learn to read, write, and spell accurately and to their highest potential.*

*Throughout many years of practice with training thousands of teachers and teaching tens of thousands of students, we've learned how to utilize EBLI to provide instruction, practice, and ongoing guidance to ensure every teacher is effectively and efficiently teaching reading, spelling, and writing to all students. This is done through in-person and online training and follow-up coaching. In addition, trainees are provided with EBLI materials, detailed lesson plans, and a jam-packed web-based support site with hundreds of instructional videos, guides, webinars, and resources.*

*As teachers teach using EBLI, they also learn how to increase purposeful student participation, support student metacognition, use real-time assessment and feedback, and promote positive classroom behavior.*

EBLI works on two complementary levels: It is an efficient and successful method of instruction for learners of all ages, including the adults we teach, *and* it addresses the problem of teacher training by providing a training method that builds teachers a solid bridge from theory to practice and application with students. Here was the final piece of the puzzle I'd so long been looking for. The John Corcoran Foundation had found a way around the gatekeepers, and we were already developing the tools to open that way up via the internet. Nora had a teaching method that worked for students of all ages and ability levels *and* a program for others to learn to teach the method, plus she had moved EBLI to online platforms through apps for student instruction and facilitated interactive online teacher training. Our next step was an obvious one; we joined forces. The collaboration between the John Corcoran Foundation's online tutoring developments and Nora Chahbazi's EBLI continues to produce deeply satisfying results. In addition, the Foundation's staff became EBLI experts by attending several EBLI training sessions in Michigan, and also hosted Nora in California and Colorado to provide EBLI training to our staff and others. Kayla Mertes Scheider, the Foundation's executive director, became a certified EBLI trainer and has since provided trainings for educators from schools throughout California.

While that model is being replaced with facilitators in the online training, the John Corcoran Foundation staff will continue to use their expertise in this capacity. Ensuring that EBLI instruction is delivered to teachers and students with fidelity is a responsibility we take very seriously.

Technology has become the way of the world, and school districts throughout the country are beginning to get the EBLI message. They too are benefitting from the EBLI online training or sending teachers of all grade levels from around the country to Michigan to be trained in EBLI instructional methodology by Nora and her staff. Even without advertisement or marketing, the word is spreading. Teachers tell teachers, their principals, and others, and district administrators are using funding to build their teachers' competency by using a system that has been shown again and again to produce astounding student gains.

Because EBLI provides practical application of knowledge for teachers to provide effective, efficient literacy instruction to their students, and because student gains with EBLI are so impressive, Marygrove College has made EBLI part of their online Masters in Reading and Masters in the Art of Teaching courses offered nationally. This is the beginning of what is ideally a trend for more colleges and universities to take advantage of EBLI's revolutionary information and instruction for their education students.

It felt like I was coming full circle at last. I once thought that learning to read would mark the end of a difficult and shame-filled period in my life, but in fact it was only the beginning of my journey. What I had been trying to do for so long was to bring every person who needed it their own Pat Lindamood. I had been so profoundly transformed by learning to read at age 48, I felt it incumbent upon me to take on the mission myself—and as arduous as it has been, fended off by gatekeepers at every pass, I nonetheless feel it a great privilege to do this work. Literacy has brought me so much, created opportunities and partnerships and journeys I'd never imagined for myself, but the lion's share of work still remains to be done.

Millions continue to be locked out of organizations that are trying to help them. Countless individuals, through one program or another, have been helped, but it is the cycle of illiteracy/sub-literacy that must be eradicated, beginning at home and with the parents who are children's very first teachers. With the easy access of the EBLI program through many avenues, including student instruction apps and online teacher training, we have a solution that has the potential to reach untold numbers of teachers and learners around the world.

I am still at heart an advocate and an activist for the prevention and eradication of adult illiteracy and sub-literacy. However, illiterate and sub-literate children become illiterate and sub-literate adults. I'm not interested in making money or chasing personal acclaim. What our years of work at the John Corcoran Foundation have led us to is not a silver bullet; it is simply a solution that works. Certainly, there are other solutions too; more power to them. The parameters of my mission came slowly to me, as a result of my evolving experiences. I'm now 79 years old and crystal clear on my mandate: to create and disseminate literacy resources. With both EBLI apps and teacher training now available online, what remains is to shout it from the rooftops. Everyone can learn to read, whether they are a 5-year-old or a senior citizen. We have a solution. You can start today.

# Time to Turn the Table
*by John Corcoran*

*Some of you may think I'm old,*
*But in my mind I'm not that old.*
*When it comes to reading, I am bold,*
*Or so, at least, I have been told.*

*And perhaps it's true that I am bold*
*Because more people must be told.*
*A teacher can never really succeed*
*Unless they teach their students to read;*

*A student can never really succeed*
*Until that student knows how to read.*
*That's one fact you must never concede:*
*The fact we all need to learn to read.*

*Street smarts and an observing eye*
*Will at times get you by,*
*But inside we know that it's a lie;*
*For something's missing behind that eye.*

*Without a full deck I played a good game,*
*But in the game of life I always felt lame.*
*You need the full deck to play your best*
*And reading's the way to pass the test.*

*I did not learn to read at eight*
*I learned to read at forty-eight,*
*And though I think that was great*
*Don't you think a man of forty-eight*
*Could have, should have, learned at eight?*

*I learned it late, but I was glad,*
*Not mad—but I'll admit I'm sad.*
*They still are using that same old label*
*Calling us learning disabled.*

*Hey, we can learn, we are able!*
*So, maybe it's time to turn the table*
*Call it right, uncloak the fable:*
*Call it true—teaching disabled.*

*Forget the shame, and stop the blame*
*Cut the cards; it's a new game*
*We know now that we're learning-abled*
*So, give up saying we're "disabled"*
*It's time to STOP with that old label.*

*It's up to us, are we able?*

## INTERLUDE: "A STUDENT ON THE ALIENATION OF LEARNING DIFFERENTLY" BY AARON WOLF

In second grade I got my first educational "gift"—the Aaron Chair. At that time, my parents had been told that my IQ was some number that was "off the charts." But the actual effort I was putting into school was on the charts, and it was way, way down at the very, very bottom. So, my teachers gave me my "gift", a chair outside the classroom where I would go every time I was distracted, misbehaved, or otherwise didn't put in the effort I should. I was in public school, and my lack of performance was made VERY public—and to everyone in the school, it was called the Aaron Chair.

I was always visual, and loved film and acting and directing. This was where I thrived. This was where I excelled. But in the classroom, I was an underachiever. I couldn't finish my books; it took me forever to read; I didn't have the patience to do memorization and homework. Throughout the rest of my schooling, I had different versions of my Aaron Chair, A.K.A. my "he's lazy" chair. It wasn't until my senior year of high school that I went to my folks and said that I was sure I had learning disabilities. Being the supportive parents that they are, they helped me follow up on my intuition, and lo and behold, I was ADHD and dyslexia-positive. No wonder I failed my driver's ed test by making a right turn when the teacher said to make a left.

Thus, the real journey began. Who is the real me? What are my real talents? How can I maximize those talents, that were otherwise being minimized in the classroom? Now, with the loving support of parents and teachers and colleagues who don't shun but instead let me shine, I am able to understand my strengths rather than exploit my weaknesses. My Aaron Chair is a place I am now very proud to sit in. My Aaron Chair is where my film career is. My Aaron Chair is where my production company is. My Aaron Chair is where my acting work, the characters I play, the commercials I'm in, the films I direct, the scripts I write—THAT is where my Aaron Chair is. And I hope everyone finds THEIR chair and gets to learn to be proud of who they are and what they can accomplish, and not be shunned into thinking that just because you are different something is wrong with you. Because it's not. You are great just the way you are. We all have an educational "gift"—and that gift is to be the best version of who WE are, to find our Chairs, to sit upright and proud and smile, and be all that we can be.

# CHAPTER NINE

# The Literacy Paradox

*M*y dubious achievements proved not to be an obstacle to college. In fact, owing to my football and basketball prowess, I was offered an athletic scholarship that covered the entire cost of my tuition, room, and board—and threw in a small stipend for laundry money. As filled with gratitude as I was, soon after my arrival on campus I began to worry that here in college, I might be in over my head. I met my new roommate, who was also an athlete, and he began to fill me in on ways in which the system worked to our advantage. Athletes avoided the rush to register for classes before they filled up (leaving you stuck with second, third, or even fourth choice,) and instead pre-registered before the rest of the student body. With that event soon approaching, I turned to my old reliable instincts.*

*Hanging around the dining hall at various tables frequented by athletes, I picked up a wealth of information merely by eavesdropping. I knew which teachers to avoid, and which I wanted to take. Then I signed up for more classes than I needed. I'd heard you could drop a class up to three weeks into the semester with no penalty. In this way, I was able to scout my professors and drop those who liked students to read aloud in class, or assigned frequent essays. Yes, it was college, but it centered around a system. And where there was a system, there was a way to get around it.*

In September of 2016, a public interest law firm based in California filed a suit against state officials in Michigan on behalf of seven students. The suit alleged that by denying students access to literacy, they had violated the students' constitutional rights. In terms of the law, the case is unprecedented. The suit, which is ongoing at the time of this writing, is structured on the argument that under the Fourteenth Amendment,

> **Universities should not have to pit academic integrity against athletic integrity.**

equal protection under the law includes students' access to an adequate education. It argues that since the state is responsible for facilitating the constitutional guarantee of equal access to education, and given that there is documented evidence to substantiate that specific schools in the Detroit system are "functionally incapable of delivering access to literacy," these students' civil rights have been violated.

As it often happens, for an injustice to be addressed in the federal legal arena on the basis of constitutionality, the specific case chosen must be extreme, egregious, and overwhelmingly condemning. The public schools in Detroit include districts with some of the lowest proficiency rates in the country. The lawsuit, *Gary B. v. Snyder*, says that "decades of state disinvestment in and deliberate indifference to Detroit schools have denied Plaintiff schoolchildren access to the most basic building block of education: literacy."

We have, as our nation's founders so eloquently put it, held these truths to be self-evident. But now, for the first time, this very issue is being raised on a federal level under the framework of the U.S. Constitution. The *Gary B. v. Snyder* complaint states that "Literacy is the foundation of all education. Experts agree that in the twenty-first century, literacy means having the ability to encode and decode language so as to access knowledge and communicate. Literacy means not only the ability to recognize or pronounce a written word, but the ability to use language to engage with the world—to understand, analyze, synthesize, reflect, and critique. Literacy development is progressive and cumulative, and literacy instruction must therefore extend throughout both primary and secondary education."

In defining the parameters of what constitutes providing access to literacy, the complaint neatly sums up ideas very familiar to the John Corcoran Foundation's stand on "Access to literacy". It reads, "requires evidence-based literacy instruction at both the elementary and secondary school levels; a stable, supported, and appropriately trained teaching staff; basic instructional materials; safe physical conditions that do not impede learning; and support for students' social-emotional needs."

Eureka! Sixty years after the *Brown v. Board of Education* ruling addressed the issue of inequity in education and the disparities visited via segregation, *Gary B. v. Snyder* produces clear evidence to prove that this inequity still exists, that it manifests along racial and economic lines, and that its effects on students in blocking their access to literacy are devastating. But the importance of the assertion reaches across those lines to every public-school system in the country. It should in no way be assumed that because this case involves a school in a poor district, illiteracy must then be a problem largely mapped by economic and racial lines; that is absolutely not the case. The plaintiff attorneys understand that litigation is always a gamble, and as such they have chosen the very worst of our schools, ones failing to serve their students in every imaginable way, in order to maximize the chances of winning a victory that will benefit everyone.

Nonetheless, the case is asserting the rights of *all* students to adequate education from properly trained teachers by shining the spotlight on the most inadequate schools in the country, and calling for the establishment of "an evidence-based, systemic approach to literacy instruction and intervention, with appropriate accountability measures." A right decision in this case would have a national impact in advancing the cause of literacy.

The prevalence of improperly trained teachers in these and other school districts is painfully clear, as is the failure of state officials to even attempt to address the problem. Instead of, as the complaint puts it, "instead of providing students with a meaningful education and literacy, the State simply provides buildings—many in serious disrepair—in which students pass days and then years with no opportunity to learn to read, write, and comprehend," and that "these schools lack the qualified teaching staff required to bring students to literacy—that is, teachers who are certified, properly trained, and assigned to a class within the area of their qualifications and expertise." It further states that a number of classes are covered by individuals with no certification whatsoever, who have no expertise in the subject at hand.

It is virtually impossible at this stage to deny that the issue of proper instruction by properly trained teachers is paramount in turning back illiteracy/sub-literacy. And there is overwhelming reason to believe that even fully certified teachers are not receiving training that is effective.

I have been accused on occasion of simply laying the blame for the illiteracy and sub-literacy epidemic on teachers, an accusation I find difficult to understand. I see the adage as "train, don't blame." Teachers are not responsible for flaws in the college and university system that leave them inadequately prepared to teach all of their students effectively. Most graduate students acquire their degrees, but aren't prepared for the workplace. They go into schools to teach when they aren't ready, burdened not only by the financial debt of their college education but by the debt of improper, ineffective instruction on how to teach reading. How, then, can it be construed as blame when it is obviously impossible to teach what one doesn't know, and impossible to use tools that one hasn't been given? That would be akin to blaming students for being sub-literate or illiterate when they had not been properly taught how to read.

The issue of teacher performance and preparedness has also been the subject of litigation, with an unexpectedly favorable result. After an 11-year battle, a Connecticut Superior Court ruling in September of 2016 found a significant section of the state's public education to be unconstitutional in the case *Connecticut Coalition for Justice in Education Funding v. Docket*. A September 7, 2016 *Wall Street Journal* article by Joseph De Avila reports that "Superior Court Judge Thomas Moukawsher ruled that the funding mechanism for public schools violated the state constitution, and ordered the state to come up with a new funding formula. He also ordered the state to set up a mandatory standard for high school graduation, overhaul evaluations for public school teachers, and create new standards for special education."

"This is a very, very big deal," said Preston Green III, professor of urban education at the University of Connecticut's Neag School of Education. "We are talking almost a total revamping of the educational system."

It is a sweeping condemnation, and as with *Gary B. v. Snyder*, the fact that it is a Connecticut ruling does not change the fact that the case has made some important gains and legitimized what so many have known for so long: "The state can't continue down the same path with troubled elementary schools.

**Current preparation programs are producing insufficiently trained teachers.**

The failure is just too big and the response to it is just too small. Therefore, the state must propose a definition of what it means to have an elementary school education that is rationally and primarily related to developing the basic literacy and numeracy skills needed for secondary school." The judge declared that too many American students graduate from high school with "illusory degrees."

The issue of the need for reform in teacher evaluations and guidelines in public schools is directly addressed in Judge Moukawsher's written decision. "The state's teacher evaluation system is little more than cotton candy in a rainstorm. Everything about it suggests it was designed to give only the appearance of imposing a significant statewide evaluation standard. These empty evaluation guidelines mean good teachers can't be recognized and bad teachers reformed or removed." In the same section, he writes, "No one defended the idea that having a master's degree makes a better teacher, and an extensive study by Jennifer King Rice shows that it has nothing to do with how well a teacher teaches. Although state officials, local board members, superintendents, principals, and teachers testified, no one said long years on the job and advanced degrees always meant good teaching."

The elephant in the room remains our inadequate qualifications for teacher credentialing. Requirements for teaching credentials vary from state to state, with most including earning a bachelor's degree followed by a teacher preparation program and a certification exam and subject-specific exam. Even within a single state, the quality and efficacy of teacher training programs can differ greatly. A 2013 report from the non-profit group the National Council on Teacher Quality rated all training programs available in California at both public and private colleges and universities. Only three of the state's 52 programs received favorable ratings, while 44 of them ranked at or below "mediocre." It has been widely acknowledged that this is a national problem, and that the current preparation programs are producing insufficiently trained teachers.

In a 2014 article in the *New York Times*, New York's education commissioner, John B. King, Jr., said, "If programs cannot make dramatic improvements, it would be far better to have fewer teacher preparation programs that are of the highest quality preparing the teachers our students need than to have a multitude of struggling programs producing candidates who are not well prepared and cannot find jobs." The problem has been clearly identified, and yet the debate continues.

In an article in the Summer 2013 edition of *Education Next,* Kate Walsh writes, "Over the last few decades, criticism of teacher preparation has shifted away from a largely academic debate to the troubling performance of American students," and that longtime experts such as G. Reid Lyon are "shocked by teacher education's refusal to train teachers to use scientifically-based reading methods." The article cites other notable critics of traditional teacher preparation, including the former dean of Columbia University's Teachers College, Arthur Levine, who is quoted as saying "Teacher education is the Dodge City of the education world. Like the fabled Wild West town, it is unruly and disordered."

Walsh identifies a shift in philosophy behind teacher education from a training model—the imparting of factual knowledge—to a formation model. In this formation model, the teaching candidate is not prepared with specific methodology, but rather with the development of a potential or "capacity" within their profession. This leaves the teaching candidate with a system structured to "launch the candidate on a lifelong path of *learning,* distinct from *knowing,* as actual knowledge is perceived as too fluid to be achievable." And as Walsh quite rightly concludes, this model, favoring generalities over specificity, is the most damaging in the realm of reading instruction.

Over the last year, the courtroom has also been the arena of disappointing news for an important and especially insidious outcome of the literacy epidemic. August of 2016 saw the dismissal of a suit filed by former University of North Carolina students and athletes, holding the NCAA partially culpable for decades of facilitation of a system in which UNC recruited star athletes, then created a phantom academic program that allowed them to meet curricular requirements while continuing to be revenue-makers for a multi-million-dollar sports program. The suit, filed the previous year, charged that neither UNC nor the NCAA had acted diligently to provide a complete quality education to athletes, making reference to the high-profile 2010 scandal at Chapel Hill.

In the 2015 book *Cheated,* Jay Smith and Mary Willingham investigate the 20-year-period during which a number of administration, faculty, and coaches created a mirage curriculum for some 1,500 athletes—enrolling them in courses with no instructor, no required meetings, and not a single written assignment for the semester. Coaches earning well over a million dollars a year are incentivized to recruit and retain the highest level of athletes, but not to educate them. Those same athletes are abandoned at graduation when they cease to be profitable, launching them into the world as college graduates in the technical sense only with utterly no preparation to function in any work arena outside of athletics.

In many colleges and universities, athletics are a significant and longstanding part of the very heart of the institution. I'm not suggesting that it would be helpful or even viable to focus reform on extricating the athletic from the academic. The system is too entrenched. What makes sense is to look once again to the single route of reform that will have the most far-reaching impact: reforming how universities teach and how they credential teachers. The effects would not be felt immediately, but if this system was successfully reformed, then all of our students—including these athletes—would be taught what they need in elementary school, long before their college years.

Universities should not have to pit academic integrity against athletic integrity.

There is no need to impart blame, then, when we can skip straight to the matter of what most needs to be done—reforming the teacher education arena. It's very clear that reform isn't going to, and likely can't, take place without the exertion of pressure from parties outside of the system. What is happening in the courtroom could be of tremendous impact, but cases of this magnitude can go on for years, or even a decade, before a final ruling is made. So what do we do now?

The onus may lie on our old reliable vehicle, the grassroots movement—a movement capable of communicating that it is time to wake up and pay attention to the contemporary scientific understanding of reading; a movement forceful enough to create a nucleus of a critical mass able to reform the foundation and approach of teacher instruction and preparation.

That's obviously a very tall order. The tendency to maintain the status quo is very deeply rooted, and in the age of consumerism that has descended on the field of education, there are the issues of money and profit—those organizations who have them obviously want to keep them. But as Judge Thomas Moukawsher so succinctly puts it in the conclusion of

**Enrollment in teacher preparation programs continues to decline while student enrollment in K–12 is on the rise.**

the *Connecticut Coalition for Justice in Education Funding v. Docket* decision, "Schools are for kids."

According to the U.S. Department of Education, between 2011 and 2021, some one and a half million new openings are or will be available for teachers to replace those who are retiring. Many of those openings will be filled by teaching candidates who have been educated and certified in traditional programs. The 2011 "Our Future, Our Teachers" plan from the Department of Education reported that 62% of new teachers felt unprepared for "classroom realities." However, the DOE also has data indicating that across the nation, enrollment in teacher preparation programs began declining in 2010 and have continued that decline. Simultaneously, student enrollment in K-12 has been projected to see a total growth spurt of 5.2% between 2011 and 2023.

There is obviously a great deal of work ahead for policymakers, for parents, for non-profits, for politicians, and for educators. In parsing all of the issues clustered under the teacher education umbrella, it is crucial to remember that we not view them in abstract or unconnected forms, but rather present and view them as interconnected factors that collectively continue to impact the illiteracy/sub-literacy epidemic. It is a simple formula of logic.

We have established the effect of illiteracy/sub-literacy on individuals, on unemployment rates, on health issues, and on crime rates, all of which collectively snowball into a millstone around the nation itself. We have established the problem of lack of effective teacher training and linked that directly to illiteracy rates in schools; and we have the data indicating a teacher shortage occurring simultaneously with a growing student population.

We can see this as a self-perpetuating cycle at every level, from the individual to the national. The child who is not learning to read in the first grade is statistically less likely to find adequate teaching in the 2nd or 5th or 7th grade; the tendency of the problem is to worsen, not to self-correct. Schools with children who are not being properly taught to read will spend more time using ineffective methodology to teach them, causing proficiency rates to drop—which can affect everything from federal funding to the pool of attractive teacher candidates. States with rising numbers of functionally illiterate and sub-literate young adults will have an increasing proportion of citizens more likely to be unemployed, to require social assistance and medical care, and who are unable to fully function in society. The effects keep spiraling outward, but the cycle of self-perpetuation is always the same.

The gains won by the decision in *Connecticut Coalition for Justice in Education Funding v. Docket* could well bring many changes that would likely reach schools across the country. If *Gary B. v. Snyder* is successful, its effect on reform could be significant. As the first legal action that is seeking to confirm a guarantee of literacy under the United States Constitution, it has the capacity to impact the issue on a national level and to establish once and for all that literacy is a civil rights issue. As such, it could become the rocket fuel that could propel a grassroots movement directly into the engine of reform.

But we don't have the luxury of waiting. We simply cannot afford it. The time to act is now.

# INTERLUDE: "THE GIFT OF LITERACY IS A GIFT TO SHARE"

*by Kayla Scheidler granddaughter of John Corcoran and former executive director of the John Corcoran Foundation*

I learned to read at four years old. I can't remember the process, but my grandparents remind me often, so it must be true.

In fourth grade, I read the book *The Teacher Who Couldn't Read* by John Corcoran, and as my book report, I invited the author to come and speak to my class.

My love for reading, language, and books (both to acquire information and open up worlds in my imagination) continue throughout my life. Learning about root words, syntax, and linguistics thrills me.

After college, I began working for the John Corcoran Foundation, a nonprofit dedicated to providing reading instruction and technology to low-income, at-risk youth. We conducted home visits for the children in our program, and as staff and reading specialists we were faced with the destruction and pain that illiteracy/sub-literacy causes in children and families.

Day after day, I met with children who could not look at me without tears in their eyes for fear that I'd ask them to read a word, parents who nervously admitted that they could not read either, gang members who'd given up on the possibility of an education, and grandparents who begged that their grandchildren be given the opportunities that they weren't offered. My heart often broke as we encountered children and adults scarred by illiteracy/sub-literacy, and many hiding their secret or pretending they did not care.

Those who struggle with reading have superb brains that simply process information differently than the way our traditional education system has chosen to teach language. The ability to read is directly correlated to all success in school, including behavioral success—which leads to self-worth, self-esteem, self-motivation, and self-responsibility.

With each child, teen, or adult we taught to read, we opened a door to freedom and possibility that did not exist before. Yet we had to reach more people. We began training teachers, who would then teach thousands of students during their careers. Teaching teachers how the brain learns to read and how to tailor instruction to each individual brain offered even more freedom and possibility.

Teaching another human to read is more rewarding than I could have ever imagined. Maybe it's my love for reading, or maybe it's just in my blood—a family legacy.

# CHAPTER TEN

# The Ticking Clock

*A fter four years of my feinting and slighting the system, it had failed to catch me. The "dumb row" dude was going to graduate from college. It was a big deal for me, and an even bigger deal for my family, as I was the first child in the family to get a college degree. They decided to make the drive from California so that they could see the ceremony for themselves. The moment itself was over in a flash. I stood surrounded by beaming family members, clutching my diploma (this one not blank) and disappointed but not surprised at how quickly my happiness was being eclipsed by anxiety. Now what? Certainly, there were many options open to me, many potential paths I could choose that would complement my strengths and abilities; and I was out of school at long last, a place that made no sense to me, a place where I made no sense at all.*

*So perhaps I made my decision to be ironic, or perhaps after 16 years of places that made no sense, I had lost what was left of mine. Because when I settled on what I wanted to do, it certainly made no sense.*

*I decided to become a teacher.*

The clock is ticking, and we have to hear it. When a child begins to fall behind in the classroom, they enter a precarious state of dropping out emotionally and psychologically. The ramifications of this state can manifest for decades, often with devastating results. While I am trying to communicate the highest level of urgency, I am also bringing good news, which is that even after many years the deeply damaging fallout of illiteracy/sub-literacy on an individual can be healed. I say that not out of optimism, but because since partnering with EBLI, we at the John Corcoran Foundation have personally witnessed this happen. I can think of no better or more inspiring example of this than a young man named Michael.

Michael was facing numerous great challenges in his life. From a very young age, because of complications from frequent seizures, the medical and educational systems believed that he lacked the ability to acquire proficient literacy and life skills. Michael was placed in "special" classes that focused on teaching life skills, such as how to do laundry, do simple cooking, maintain hygiene, and communicate properly instead of the academic classes other children his age attended.

As with so many young people who are not taught to read and write, Michael developed a deep sense of anger and began to act out his rage, which was his only remaining avenue of communication. The school's response was to control Michael by literally locking him out of the school building. He was further stressed by poor health, suffering from repeated seizures and the side effects of over 30 medications. At the age of 20, he underwent an operation to remove a portion of the left temporal lobe of his brain that was the origin of his seizures. Following the surgery, the seizures he'd had since birth—sometimes up to 50 a day, each lasting under 60 seconds—disappeared, as did the exhaustion that accompanied them. After the operation, Michael was able to stay awake, and became aware that he was different than other people in that he did not have the tools to read or to navigate life.

This became unbearable for him, and he attempted suicide. Again, like so many of his peers suffering from illiteracy, Michael's desperation drove him to make bad choices, and he ultimately was incarcerated. Upon being released, he returned to school; in Michigan, districts are required to provide education until the age of 26 to those who haven't graduated. When he was 25, Michael's school agreed to pay for outside instruction until he was 26 if his mother promised to remove him from the school. In their opinion, Michael was unteachable and irredeemable. But his mother, Michelle, had no intention of giving up on him. She took him to EBLI's Ounce of Prevention Reading Center, and that is when our worlds intersected.

When Michael first came to the center, he'd been weaning off over 30 medications to prevent seizures and treat mood swings, anxiety, and agitation. He was still in the court system, attending mental health court appointments weekly. He could only read the word "is," and he couldn't write at all. After two decades of being effectively written off in school and marginalized by most of society, his fury was barely contained. His eyes blazed with rage.

> **After EBLI instruction a significant improvement in reading and cognitive ability can be achieved.**

Two years later, after 100 hours of EBLI instructional classes, Michael is a very different person. He can read at almost a 7th grade level and he can write. He has a part-time job. He is no longer in the court system. He is completely off all but two of his medications, and the rage in his eyes has disappeared completely, replaced by a deep-seated kindness and optimism that make him a delight to be around. As Michael himself puts it, learning to read "makes me feel reborn." For years, Michael had carried a sense of shame that was so deeply rooted it seemed to be a permanent part of him, something he was born with. When he learned to read and write the shame lifted, and it was only with hindsight that he was able to understand how heavily the burden of illiteracy had pressed on him, leaving scars on virtually every aspect of his life.

Under those circumstances, a person could not be blamed if they became bitter at having been pushed off the educational path and abandoned without the most necessary skill in modern society—the ability to read and write. A person could not be blamed for dwelling on all the lost time, all the vanished opportunities stolen from them in their childhood. But Michael is not that person. In the great space in Michael that was once filled with shame, a flame of fierce pride has been kindled. The frustration and agitation that were once his constant companions gave way to determination and motivation, and the fuel that powers him now is his own direct understanding that the payoff is guaranteed— where in the past he had been hypnotized into believing that many things were "impossible" for him. He continues to become more and more open to what he can do, as opposed to what he is not capable of. Once terrified that the secret of his illiteracy would be found out, Michael now more freely shares his story with others in the hopes of inspiring them by his example. He wants to eventually learn to teach others to read.

Michael's story touches on many of the fundamental territories covered in this book. His rightful place in the classroom was denied him by the gatekeepers, who hastily labeled him "learning disabled" and decided he was unteachable. He became one of countless innocent victims of the blame-free disability culture. In an era in which technology had already yielded significant understanding of the human brain and provided proof that reading is an acquired skill, not a fixed function of intelligence, and that no two brains adapt to accommodate the process of reading in bewildering and humiliating time, Michael was simply shut out of exactly the same way, educators in Michael's life still clung to an outdated one-size-fits-all method of teaching.

Caught in the endless loop of labeling, Michael's "learning disability" became a self-fulfilling prophecy. Hypnotized by the adults and authority figures in his life who believed he couldn't learn, Michael couldn't learn. Faced with the constant message that he was "bad" and destined for "failure", Michael became bad; he failed. He became his phantom diagnosis, and his own sense of personhood was consumed by a toxic cloud of anger. He reached adulthood and unknowingly joined the ranks of millions of American adults who cannot read or write.

Over-medicated and under-taught, Michael had been prevented from receiving the education constitutionally guaranteed to him, leaving him unable to earn a living or survive within the confines of the law. Following the statistic likelihood, he ended up in prison and emerged angrier and more hopeless than ever before. And yet in spite of it all, regardless of everything that had marked him over the years and decades, the damage was still reversible. All he had to do was to seek help in the last place logic dictated it would be: *outside* the educational system.

When Michael and his mother found EBLI and the Ounce of Prevention Reading Center, the once unteachable, unreformable, unmanageable, and unwelcome student learned to read and write. The myth of Michael's life began to unravel, and he reclaimed the personhood that illiteracy had denied him. With the help of dedicated professionals, of advocates and time-proven methodology coupled with technology, Michael began to cultivate a sense of pride and a powerful work ethic he never knew he had.

Michael can never get back those lost years, but in stepping into the person he was born to be, he has much less time or inclination for bitterness today. Instead, he is excited about the future, and all the possibilities it holds for him—possibilities he once believed did not exist for people like him. What better news could there possibly be? Part of my life's work has become shouting it from the rooftops. But like all truly good news, it tends to be lost in the stasis of bureaucracy, policy, blame, and debate.

In 2013, I appeared in a beautiful little film made by the San Diego Council on Literacy. It was titled *Voices and Faces—Literacy in San Diego*, and it featured interviews with a number of people (myself included) who had not learned to read and write until adulthood. The voices and faces captured in that film are of men and women, young and old, working class and white-collar, privileged and underprivileged—people from every walk of life, every culture you can imagine. It is a vivid reminder that the epidemic of illiteracy/sub-literacy crosses all barriers of income, upbringing, race, and gender.

In the film's opening credits, it quotes the San Diego Literacy Council's mission statement, "Uniting the community to support literacy through leadership, advocacy, and resources." As I consider these words now that I am approaching the end of writing my *Literacy Manifesto*, I am struck not just by their power, but by the fact that the words themselves encompass what I have come to believe are the most crucial aspects of the illiteracy solution. That realization makes me want to look more closely at them, because if I've come to know anything in my 79 years, it is that words are magical and mysterious and endlessly fascinating. When a culture or nation wants to better understand itself, and glimpse where it's been and where it's going, a simple and enlightening means to this end is to study its words and their origins.

**UNITE** (from the Latin *unit,* "joined together," and the Latin *unus,* "one.") This is a call for unity. Our nation was built on the principle that in uniting, we have more power and prosperity than when we are separate. Educators, policymakers, volunteers, parents, pediatricians, librarians, counselors—they are all vital parts of a unified whole. Together, committed to a desire for universal literacy, we can provide proven instructional programs to anyone, anywhere, who needs them.

**COMMUNITY** (from the Latin *communis,* "belonging to all.") This is a call for communities of all kinds to take action to end the epidemic of illiteracy/sub-literacy. Churches, parks and recreation departments, library boosters, mentoring groups, veteran's organizations, political clubs, Scouts and 4H groups: they belong to us all, and each one is a venue of our own local community able to best reach individuals who aren't functionally literate and likely unaware that a simple, easy-to-use solution is already available in the here and now.

**SUPPORT** (from the Latin *supportare,* "to convey, carry, bring up, bring forward.") This is a call to go back and carry forward those who were silently abandoned. There is no shame in acknowledging how many students were left behind, not being taught how to read, if we are willing to take the action of bringing them forward. It costs us nothing, and we have so much to gain.

**LEADERSHIP** (from the Old English *lædan*, "to guide, conduct.") This is a call for leaders who can guide us. The change to universal literacy needs a great variety of leaders of all kinds—volunteers, pioneers, dedicated professionals, activists, lobbyists, politicians, teachers, mentors, doctors, and businesspeople. Whether you choose to take on the Constitution or to share a petition, your leadership is desperately needed.

**ADVOCATE** (from the Latin *advocare*, "to call to one's aid.") This is a call to advocate for those who are unable to do it for themselves. For many people who cannot read, shame and fear of stigmatization make seeking help unthinkable.

**RESOURCE** (from the Latin *resurgere*, "to rise again.") This is a call to rise. Illiteracy drags down individuals and families, communities and nations. It is a civil rights violation of staggering proportions, and a tragedy all the more telling in the face of our widespread acknowledgment that the education system is failing our children and all the more unthinkable in the face of the knowledge that effective instructional methods are easily and cheaply available right now.

With the understanding of the antiquity and the roots of each of these words, they resonate even more powerfully: "Uniting the community to support literacy through leadership, advocacy, and resources." As I reach the end of this book, there is one more word that it feels right to examine.

**MANIFESTO** (from the Latin *manifesto*, "to make public.") This is a manifesto of an obvious yet stubbornly elusive truth: everyone deserves to know how to read and write. Everyone. No one is born with the inherent inclination to cheat or to lie. No boy or girl finishes their first day of kindergarten with the desire to be relegated to the modern equivalent of the "dumb row," or to be singled out as a problem child. No one strives to be marginalized, disenfranchised, or stigmatized. No one seeks to take on the suffocating burden of shame. No one wants to be sub-literate. No one wants to be left behind. And yet it happens every day. It has likely happened to someone in your family, or someone that you know. It happened to me.

They say God works in mysterious ways; who could have imagined that Johnny from Dumb Row would ultimately devote his life to advocating teaching the skills of reading and writing? For that and many other reasons, I cannot say that I would change my experience if I had the power to, that I would go back in time and be a reading, writing student—a good boy with good grades and good prospects. I am not sure that I would change my acquaintance with the experience of illiteracy, or my journey in becoming and then transcending "the teacher who couldn't read." I am not sure that I could or would give up the extraordinary places my work has taken me or the exciting opportunities and remarkable people it has brought my way. The good and most precious aspects of my life are hopelessly entangled with the bad, and it is all a part of who I have become. I was one of too many people who were not taught what they needed to know in school, and I was one of too few people who eventually *did* learn with the help of others outside of the educational system. I know that my story is not an unusual one; I know that the illiteracy epidemic did not begin with me.

But, if I could be granted one wish it would be that it ends with me.

# Epilogue

*By Way of a Eulogy*

**EULOGY**—(from the Latin *eulogium* and the Greek *eulogia*, "praise; good or fine language").

**PRAISE**—good or fine language. I cannot think of a more perfect ending.

*I have put much of my heart and my soul into this* Literacy Manifesto—*the last word, if you will, that I will leave the literacy community and those outside of it. The process of writing this book stirred up deep maelstroms of emotion within me. I began to realize how much shame I still carried with me. I began to recognize a feeling I had never been able to name, a feeling that would come upon me and lodge deep and heavy in my gut, a feeling that something needed to be done. Something needed to happen. Gradually, I came to know that feeling as a particular manifestation of my shame. I came to see it was not so much a feeling as a need, a longing. And eventually, I found I had come to a pretty good idea of what that longing was for.*

*Reconciliation.*

Contrition.

Liberation.

After everything—from facing my fears and asking for help to publicly confessing my sins in my book *The Teacher Who Couldn't Read*, after thirty years of devoting every spare hour to the issue of literacy, even after founding the John Corcoran Foundation to further that work—I was still ashamed of myself. It was almost crippling at times, and I know it perplexed my wife and the few people around me who know how deeply entrenched I was in that shame. To me, those truths were self-evident. I had cheated and lied to get through school, cheated and lied to graduate from college, cheated and lied to teach. I'd been an athlete all that time, and no athlete worth his salt wants to cheat to win; no athlete worth his salt would be comfortable with a trophy presented for a game in which anyone on his team had cheated.

During all the work that went into this book, I felt those biographical sketches at the beginning of each chapter were about a ghost of the past, a shadow of a version of me now gone for some thirty long years. I felt that during the writing, we would be burying that ghost right here in these pages. But as the process led me to relive what the days were like for that ghost living in a sub-culture for five decades without knowing or understanding the language of the culture, and to recall how much that ghost suffered under the dark internal cloud of fear and insecurity that were his constant companions, then it didn't feel like the ghost was being buried at all. Because I felt myself under that dark cloud too, and I suffered, and I felt pain. Why was I still so vulnerable to those feelings? I began to feel a little desperate that there must be a way to have it done with once and for all—to set things right.

And while I understood the logic of what those close to me said—that I had more than atoned for any wrongdoing by coming clean about my past and devoting myself to help other struggling readers—while I got that their words made sense, the shame was still there inside me, raw and exposed like a nerve ending. I was most aware of that shame when the heavy feeling in my gut would manifest, that longing to set things right, to do something that would allow me to close the book on my past and be free of it.

The idea of reconciliation had been with me since my Catholic childhood catechisms. If you are deeply sorry for something, you must make a true confession. With my very deep belief in confession, this idea of reconciliation seemed to be rattling the cage of my catechism. *Forgive us our trespasses, as we forgive those who trespass against us.* And was that not exactly the sin I had committed? I had trespassed onto campus; each day that I was there, each year, I was trespassing. I did not have the required skills to be there, and I navigated my classes and won my degree through deceit. *Forgive us our trespasses.* That is when the idea came to me: I would write to my friend, now the University of Texas at El Paso's President, and I would offer to return my degree and diploma for the reason that it was obtained through false means. I had trespassed.

Many people, after receiving their diplomas, tuck them into a box or a bookshelf, and don't really think about them again. Some people frame their diplomas and proudly display them in their offices or homes. To a small group of people, the diploma is one of their most precious possessions—not because of what it says about their brain, but because of what it says about the importance of that accomplishment to them, and likely because they achieved it in the face of considerable odds. The thought of returning my diploma had flickered through my mind a number of times over the years, but I had always rejected it, feeling I couldn't possibly let my diploma go. It was too important to me. But now, as I worked on this book, the idea came to me again, and I knew at once that I had to give my diploma back.

This suddenly seemed enormously important to me, so in the earliest days of spring I sat in my office, typing the letter. I printed it on my stationery because it seemed too important a letter to just e-mail, addressed and stamped the envelope, and sent it off to Texas. This is what it said.

*Dr. Diana Natalicio, President*
*UTEP*
*500 W. University Avenue*
*El Paso, TX 79968*

*Dear Dr. Natalicio:*

*I hope this letter finds you well. I've been blessed to live a healthy life. I am presently recovering from a successful knee replacement surgery. I marvel at today's medical science and man's ability to implement it!*

*My wife Kathleen and I recently celebrated our 50th wedding anniversary. Also, the 100th birthday of my beloved UTEP was this year, as was the 50th anniversary of Texas Western College's 1966 NCAA Basketball Championship—the "Road to Glory," an achievement in which I am proud to have played a part. Charlie Brown was my friend, my teammate, and my roommate when our team traveled.*

*The UTEP story is a great story to tell the world. Under your leadership, Dr. Natalicio, UTEP has been a gateway to helping students earn their degrees and achieve social and economic success. Many of your students have been the first in their proud families to graduate from college. I was one of those students 60 years ago.*

*However, and here we reach the complicated crux of the issue about which I am writing to seek your advice, I did not earn my B.S. degree legally. You are already aware that during my entire career at TWC, I was functionally illiterate. I satisfied the requirements for a degree by using every hook and crook I could imagine and implement to pass a course. I cheated. I have publicly admitted that fact many times over.*

*You have inspired and motivated me to be a proactive literacy advocate for the past 30 years. I have had a successful life, and in that way I have brought a measure of honor to UTEP. Nevertheless, there is a gray cloud over my collegiate years at TWC that still haunts me.*

*It is unfinished business that I would like to deal with, but I know of no precedent.*

*What I propose is something like the following: Since the degree I received so long ago was "earned" by unorthodox means, I would like to give it back to the University. Exactly what this would entail I am not certain, since I have never heard anyone volunteer to "give back" a degree. However, under the circumstances, returning the degree not only seems in order, it also fills a necessary measure for satisfying my conscience.*

*Furthermore, I think that such a measure, undertaken in the right spirit, would create an opportunity to tell the UTEP story in a novel way. If I "gave back" my degree, we could use the occasion as a positive and newsworthy event. The fact that I did not earn my degree in the way others do does not negate the fact that my career at TWC was an indispensable formative period in my life, and I have gone on, as a nationally known and respected literacy advocate, to do a certain amount of good in the world due in large part to the excellence of the education I received (while not "earning" a degree) from Texas Western College.*

*I would welcome the opportunity to honor UTEP, to honor you, and to honor literacy itself on the occasion of the return of the kind I have here proposed. I realize that the technicalities of such a matter are beyond my personal expertise, so I appeal to you to advise me whether this is feasible and desirable at all, or—from your perspective and the perspective of UTEP—advisable.*

*I appreciate your consideration of this unusual proposal, and look forward to hearing from you at your convenience.*

*Sincerely,*

*John Corcoran*

I waited with some anticipation for her response, and was perplexed and a little concerned as the weeks passed with no response forthcoming. (I would later learn that Diana had been absent from campus for a significant period of time and only found my letter, along with many stacks of correspondence, waiting for her on her return.) As I checked the mail each day and found nothing, I remained optimistic that she would respond when she could, and would have a favorable view of my request. I truly felt that was all I needed to achieve the liberation I so deeply craved. It's not that I imagined the act of returning my degree as some kind of panacea. The first lesson of liberation required the peaceful acceptance of the fact that I would never be accepted by everyone. I had struggled with that, too, over the years, trying to move people to hear my message, and to understand; and not all of them did, and that was okay. I was going to be okay.

In early May, her letter in response finally arrived.

*University of Texas at El Paso*
*Office of the President*

*Dear John:*

*As always, it was good to hear from you. My apologies for the delay in responding, but I'm still catching up with the backlog of messages and correspondence that arrived during my absence from the campus.*

*Congratulations to you and your wife Kathleen on your 50th wedding anniversary! This has indeed been a semester of celebrations, with the 50th anniversary of Texas Western College's 1996 NCAA Men's Basketball Championship among the most prominent. Although I very much regretted not being able to participate in the festivities in Houston, I greatly enjoyed watching the video of the NCAA half-time tribute to our Miners during Final Four Weekend. Wonderful!*

*I continue to appreciate and be impressed by your work as a prominent literacy advocate over the past 30 years, and I congratulate you once again for shining a spotlight on this important issue. Although I believe I understand your desire to remove the "gray cloud" that you say hovers over your Texas Western College years, I don't think that returning to UTEP the TWC degree that you received 60 years ago is likely to add honor to what you've already achieved.*

*Moreover, I think it would be inappropriate for me, as UTEP's president in 2016, to participate in calling into question the judgment of individuals who were involved in assessing the quality of your performance 60 years ago. The fact is that you have very publicly atoned for your "unorthodox means" of completing your degree and made your story newsworthy for the past 30 years. Most importantly, your lifetime commitment has enabled thousands of people who have been touched by your story to see sunshine and hope, not the gray cloud that apparently continues to haunt you.*

*Thanks again for your continued commitment to serve as a literacy advocate. I hope that your recovery from knee replacement surgery continues to go well.*

*Go Miners!*

*Diana Natalicio,*
*President*

As I read her lovely and graciously kind letter, with its soft deflection of my request, I thought at first I had failed again. I had devised this action to take, to be upright, set things straight, so that I would have liberation—peace. But Dr. Natalicio's letter explained very clearly why this was neither necessary nor appropriate, and then I knew that she was quite right.

So, I kept my diploma, and my academic credentials. And the feeling of liberation I'd so longed for, the opening up of my soul, finally came. Not all at once, in a "road to Damascus" moment, but gradually and consistently, a growing space in my heart to accommodate this gentle peace.

My ultimate realization was that the important thing I had to do was not to *return* my diploma. It was to *offer* to do it, to genuinely communicate my desire to physically send it back. It was to hear Dr. Natalicio's wise response—to understand that if she accepted my offer it would be a tacit condemnation of those who judged me to be proficient. That tacit condemnation of judgments made sixty years ago certainly was inappropriate, as she so wisely said—not because of a presumption of innocence, but because, by virtue of the known circumstances, it is almost certainly true. Understanding washed over me like the light of a sunrise. From my very youngest years, my teachers had failed to teach me to read, and then they had failed to recognize this fact. In my teens, in high school, and in college, I found ways around the system and ways to hide my sub-literacy. But why did the academic system have no means to catch me in my deception? My gifts as an athlete were the qualities that won me acceptance and a full scholarship to college. How could my college professors have failed to notice that I couldn't read?

I had carried my own shame and pain for so long, but never thought to apportion it to any of the teachers who failed to teach me. The cost of their failure was severe, and I had become so caught up in guilt about the deceit I employed to stay in school in spite of my deficiency, I had forgotten the simple fact that I did not meander into sub-literacy of my own free will and volition. I went to school expecting to learn to read, just like the other kids. Yes, there were many, many wrongs, but not all of them were mine. *Forgive us our trespasses, as we forgive those who trespass against us.* One of the most powerful elements of Christianity is its focus on reciprocity, whether it is God to human or human to human. I had become so busy cultivating what I felt was shame of the unforgiveable, I had forgotten how important it was to extend forgiveness. I had forgotten how much power there is in giving someone the thing that you most want for yourself. As St. Francis said, "It is in giving that we receive, it is in pardoning that we are pardoned." And did I forgive the educators who had let me slip through the cracks? It didn't even bear much thought. We didn't know then what we do now; my elementary school teachers had no troubleshooting manual. They had been trained to teach reading in one way, and were told it would always work; and it didn't. Could I forgive them? Of course I could. Of course I did.

And now comes the long-awaited moment, here, just a few lines from the end of this book. I forgive and am forgiven, and a door swings open and I walk outside.

If Dr. Natalicio's response to me became something of an epiphany, my letter to her came to feel like a eulogy I prepared for that ghost of myself, haunting me from so many years in the past, so that he could melt peacefully into the mists of time and I could go my own way at last—my duty to him discharged in the fullest, my yoke easy and my burden light.

# Acknowledgments

In the decades since I learned to read, hundreds, if not thousands of people have assisted me in this "noble and righteous" cause of literacy for everyone. It would take me many pages to acknowledge them all. They are dedicated. They are brave. They have fire in their hearts to help prevent the replication of my traumatic experience with literacy until the age of 48. I want to deeply thank each and every one of them.

When I was a schoolboy, my sweet mother would awaken me and my five sisters by gently wiggling our feet and saying in a soft voice, "It's time." She repeated this gentle effort two or three times until we got out of our slumber and our beds.

It is time. The time is now for all of us to nudge others, gently or a bit more vigorously if need be, to tell them, "Wake up. Please. Shake off your slumber and get engaged in America's most important educational, civil, and human rights issue. LET'S TEACH ALL OF AMERICA TO READ."

# About the Author

John Corcoran's professional career represents a merger of his life as a teacher, real estate investor, builder and developer, and passionate advocacy for a literate America. His background in teaching demonstrates his continual commitment to sharing his knowledge and experience with others.

The Honorable John Corcoran was appointed to the National Institute for Literacy by President Bush and was confirmed by the U.S. Senate. Subsequently, he served on the Advisory Board of the Institute under President Bush and President Clinton. He has testified to the U.S. Congress Sub-Committee on Early Childhood Education and Family, also to the Sub-Committee on Oversight and Investigation for the Committee on Economic & Education Opportunities. In addition, he has served on numerous advisory commissions and corporate boards, has been a board member of the San Diego Council on Literacy and a member of the Executive Board on the Literacy Network of Greater Los Angeles. John is also the author of the book *The Teacher Who Couldn't Read* and *The Bridge to Literacy*.

John's responsibilities in the building and development process involved interfacing with investors, lenders, attorneys, accountants, government agencies, architects, engineers, contractors, and brokers. John's entrepreneurial spirit and management experience have been well represented in his various professional roles over the fast fifty years.

John is also a nationally known and respected speaker and lecturer who has given presentations in forty-four states, in Canada and Europe. Audiences include students, professional and volunteer teachers, teacher candidates, service groups, volunteer organizations, policy makers, and prison inmates. Numerous small businesses and Fortune 500 companies have been addressed. He has appeared on 20/20, The Oprah Winfrey Show, Larry King Live, Phil Donahue, CNN, Fox News, and ESPN. In all, he has done over 200 radio and television interviews. John was the recipient of a Lifetime Achievement Award at the 2002 Literacy Media Awards, an Encore Purpose Prize Fellow, the NCL Literacy Leadership Award recipient 2011, The Daily Points of Life Award winner 2016 along with numerous other awards over the years.

John's independent voice is rooted in his own incredible personal story and his passion for informing, challenging, and inspiring others, from political leaders to gang members. For these people and everyone in between, his message is simple: it is never too late to improve one's literacy skills. The key to teaching a child, a teen, or an adult is proper instruction. And proper instruction is delivered by properly trained teachers.

John is the founder and President/CEO of the John Corcoran Foundation Inc., a non-profit organization whose mission is to facilitate the prevention and eradication of illiteracy in adults and children across America. He and his wife have lived in Oceanside, California for over 50 years. They have two children and six grandchildren.

Visit: JohnCorcoranFoundation.org

# A Note from One of Time Magazine's 2016 100 Most Influential People in the World

John,

Thank you for sending along to me the review of your latest book and the truly eloquent and touching epilogue. I am so pleased to know that you are finally at peace with your Texas Western College degree.

*Dr Diana Natalicio*
*UTEP President*
*Time Magazine's 100 most influential people, 2016*

CPSIA information can be obtained
at www.ICGtesting.com
Printed in the USA
FSOW01n1859251117
41548FS